Women,
LEAD!

Presented by Pennsylvania Family Publishing

The creator of
Leadership Academy for Women
Beth Caldwell
presents:

Women,
LEAD!

Permissions

Women, LEAD! is an advice and information book for women who want to be influential leaders at work, at home, and in the community. If you find the content and strategies helpful and want to share them with your readers, listeners, followers, friends, family, and colleagues, please do so!

Permission to share brief excerpts or concepts from this book is granted as long as you include the following statement in full:

This content is excerpted from the book **Women, LEAD!** written by Beth Caldwell. Copies are available in bookstores and online.
Learn more at **CoachBethCaldwell.com**.

Interior and Cover Design by Daniel Szwedko Graphics

Author Photo by Mike Redford, Redford Photography
Bio photo by Amir Fathalian, Amir Media Group

To order bulk copies of **Women, LEAD!**; contact Pennsylvania Family Publishing at (412) 202-6983.

NOTICE

The information contained in this book is not intended as a substitute for the knowledge, skill, and judgment of qualified psychiatrists, psychologists, physicians, health care, holistic, wellness, or other practitioners or professionals.

Advice given is offered solely from the personal experiences of the author and is provided without specific knowledge or training in mental health or medical treatments.

Always seek the advice of a qualified health or mental health professional before making important changes or decisions. The author, Beth Caldwell, and publisher, Pennsylvania (PA) Family Publishing assume no responsibility for actions taken as a result of the content of this or any other joint publication.

Additional notes from the author:

This book contains discussion and advice about leadership and personal issues. Understand that these opinions are based on my own experiences, training, and knowledge. This advice is not intended to be used as a substitute for advice from a qualified mental health or medical professional.

Within this book, there are examples and stories from the many client interactions I've experienced in my career as a leadership consultant and life coach. To ensure their privacy and confidentiality I have changed the names and minor details. The examples from my personal life have not been altered.

Acknowledgments

I'd like to acknowledge the women who have mentored me by example. Your confidence, courage, and willingness to take risks encouraged me to do the same. Thank you!

Ali Brown
Brooke Castillo
Susan Hyatt
Lindsey Smith
Doreen Rainey
Patrice Washington
Robin Hallett
Molly Patrick
Michelle Obama
Marie Forleo
Thelma Wells
Mary Kay Ash
Arianna Huffington
Tara Mohr
Laurie Anne King
Kim Fulcher

Men's honorary mention:
Steve Harvey, Tom Volkar, and John Lee Dumas

Your work is important. Each of you have made a difference to me.
Thank you all.

Beth

Beth Caldwell

Dedication

This book is dedicated to all of the graduates of Leadership Academy for Women. You are strong and intelligent role models. Keep influencing.

Table of Contents

Introduction

A number of years ago I was doing a freelance writing job at a health care business run by a female CEO. I was in my early 30's and completely in awe of this woman and what she had achieved. She was the first female executive that I'd been exposed to and I was especially impressed with her accomplishments. She did not have a degree from a prestigious university, did not have a wealthy husband and did not inherit the business from her father. She attended a career training program to work as a medical caregiver and began working for $12/hour in the small town where she grew up. Recognizing how much rural families struggled with accessing quality health care, she had a vision and took a risk. Using her trailer as collateral, she borrowed money to buy a van that took health care practitioners to rural areas and began serving patients. Her risk paid off. Ten years later, she had more than 50 vans on the road across three states, more than 300 employees, and was earning a cool 15 million dollars in profits per year. I was hired to write press releases, website content, and community newsletters. I was thrilled just being in the same room as her. It was my dream to work with women leaders and influencers.

Usually not a morning person, I arrived early to work my first day, eager to get started. It turned out to be a disappointment. I spent most of the morning waiting outside of her office listening to her arguing with her accountant. The second day I shadowed her as she did a new employee orientation. We drove in her Mercedes, stopped for pricey coffee and she complained bitterly about the government threatening to raise the minimum wage. I remember thinking that she must have forgotten what it was like to live on $12/hour. Later I was surprised when she proudly revealed that her employees were paid less than what she earned 10 years ago.

On the third morning, there was a news report about health

care reform and the new requirements that would soon be placed upon small business owners. It played loudly on the large TV in the reception area outside of her office. I was shocked by what happened next. She screamed, stomped, and threw a chair across the room. She shouted, "I'm not paying for health care! I'll shut down this whole operation before I pay for any health benefits!" She then stomped to a bookshelf near the administrator's desk and toppled it over, scattering books, plants, and awards across the floor. A small plaque landed near my feet. I picked it up. Ironically it read "Young Business Leader of the Year Award."

The room was silent. I looked around. Her all-female staff kept their heads down, nervously pretending that nothing was happening. Most likely they were in fear of losing their jobs. I left later that morning and did not return. I remember telling my family, "If that is what being a woman leader is, I'm not interested."

Fortunately, I used this experience as training on how NOT TO LEAD. Since then, I've been blessed to meet and work with many conscientious and emotionally intelligent leaders.

Women today have the opportunity to lead others in a responsible manner. Workplaces struggle with temper tantrums, harassment, under-earning, and unethical leadership. Employees without the skills or courage to speak up or make change silently endure and cope.

As a female leader today, it's a part of your legacy to influence change and show others how to do the same. I can't wait to see what's possible!

Beth Caldwell

Warning:

Unfamiliar feelings of pride and accomplishment may begin to occur once you drop masculine productivity protocols and begin doing your work with intention.

Chapter One
Commitment to Time Mastery

Whether you're leading a corporate team of hundreds, managing a busy household, or combining a career with your family of fur babies; how you choose to manage your life and your time affects everyone around you. If you're overbooked, overwhelmed, working all the time, and not completing your projects, you come across as scattered and inefficient. You're likely to be less effective than colleagues and probably passed over for promotions. Worst of all, you will not be recognized for achievements or gain the respect of your team. I have good news for you, though: **These productivity issues are habits, and habits can be changed.**

In order to solve productivity issues, women often try to implement new programs, add rigid protocols, or embark on complicated systems to organize tasks and schedules. Sometimes the answer is not what you need to start doing, it's what you need to stop doing.

My Leadership Academy students often discover that they are subconsciously sabotaging their productivity. During class, we take a careful look at how they lose track of time and fail to leverage themselves. This realization sometimes causes shame and embarrassment, but here is your second piece of good news: **Awareness is the first step in changing these habits.**

I'm going to share with you the six most common productivity mistakes happening in the workforce today. These are the

1

exact tools given to Leadership Academy graduates to help them enhance their own productivity.

Productivity Mistake Number One: Being a Time Optimist

Time Optimism is a life-management disorder that is very common for people-pleasers and over-achievers. How many of these symptoms do you have?

Check all that apply:

☐ I tend to take on more responsibilities than are realistically possible for a person to achieve in one day/week/month/ year.

☐ I assume that I can complete tasks in a FLASH and tend to not schedule enough time to do the work well.

☐ I often forget to allow time for delays or complications when planning a project.

☐ I multi-task every day.

☐ I frequently skip meals, work late into the evenings or on weekends and sleep less than I should in order to complete the work I've committed to.

☐ I count on "no traffic" when traveling to meetings, the airport, etc.

☐ I put more tasks on my calendar than anyone else in my office.

☐ I expect myself to be able to accomplish more than I would ever expect of anyone else.

If you've checked three or more boxes, you are an over-achieving time optimist. You share this condition with lots of other high-functioning, successful people who, like you, have high standards. You have the tendency to prioritize work over your personal life and health. Even though you get a lot of work done, you're not as effective as you could be.

I struggled with time-optimism for years. The negative consequences affected me both personally and professionally. Over the years I tried changing my habits by implementing strict rules, hiring accountability coaches and being hard on myself. Those tactics failed. What works better for me is to be more intentional with my planning. Intentional planning is a very simple solution that works well. Be aware, though, if you have been a time optimist for most of your life, changing this habit will take some patience.

Here is how I did it:

1. I made the decision that I no longer wanted to be living in reactive mode, constantly responding to other people's problems. I no longer wanted to feel scattered or miss deadlines. I was ready to enjoy a healthy integration with work, family and social activities. I wanted my workdays to begin and end at normal times, and to feel fulfilled instead of exhausted at the end of the day.

2. I took responsibility for my choices that resulted in a fast paced, frantic and hectic schedule. I then created some strategies to avoid overbooking and overcommitting myself. I established realistic guidelines around how many people to meet with face to face in a day, how many phone calls I could really get done in 30 minutes, and blocked off time for meals and other breaks. If I had an engagement at 7 am, then I did not book myself an appointment for 7 pm the same day, and if working late in the evening, I did not schedule any appointments for early the next morning. It took some courage to set these boundaries but the end result was absolutely worth it.

3. To stay on track, I created a reminder that would appear on my digital calendar twice a day. It said:

- Writing
- Publicity
- Lunch and breaks every day
- Personal care and appointments
- Team member meetings for all delegated tasks

I also marked off times in the year ahead for personal and professional development workshops and education, planned family events or vacations, and a few well-placed long weekends throughout the year.[2]

I now have a calendar blueprint that provides the structure I needed but allows the flexibility that is important to me. Now, instead of saying to a client, "When would you like to meet?" I say, "I can meet on Wednesday at 11 am. Does that work for you?" This refined approach sends the message of a competent leader instead of a scattered people-pleaser.

Productivity Mistake Number Three: Solving Problems That Aren't Yours

My clients are mostly women leaders. In them, I see a constant characteristic, the need to step in and solve issues that don't belong to them. That's not leading. That's controlling. "But wait", you say, "I'm not being controlling, I'm being helpful. They NEEEED me."

My friend, the truth is that you have trained them to depend on you. You've gone above and beyond, learned all the systems, all the processes, and how to solve every problem. You have made yourself invaluable. If you own your own business, you're so busy doing work and fixing problems that you have no time to grow the business.

If you work at a corporation, you have trained others to rush to you for answers. They check with you before making decisions. It's nice to feel needed. Think about it, though. Being

invaluable prevents you from being promoted and holds the company hostage. When everyone depends on one person to make all the decisions and handle all the issues, future leaders get no chance to learn how to make important decisions. Their talents go untapped. They may get bored and move on. And the worst news: YOU don't get raises or promotions. Why pay you more if you're already being paid to do everything?

Being invaluable is another way that women sabotage their success. We don't see men running around solving other people's problems, do we? Typically men at work don't spend their time worrying about how their co-workers are performing because that is not their job. Men are very good at keeping those boundaries. They see no need to get involved or try to control every outcome. They assume that if someone isn't doing their job it will be reflected in the end result and they don't worry about the outcome. Women are wired to support. We can't help but worry about the end results. It's in our DNA. It feels completely natural to get involved, help out and give extra. This natural tendency is sabotaging our careers.

I remember being very upset when I realized that I was hurting myself with this "helpful" habit. I spent years over-performing at my job at a social services agency. I saw myself as devoted, caring and an excellent performer. The difficult truth was that I had created a big mess, one where every team member came to me for ideas and solutions. I had become depleted, exhausted and burned out. That was a tough leadership lesson, but I never made that mistake again.

Here is how I did it:

1. By incorporating time-blocking and "do not disturb" periods into my days, I discovered that when left alone, people began to solve their problems without me.

2. When folks came to me with an issue, instead of

immediately giving them options to try, I asked them a question instead.

Something like this:
- What have you tried?
- What do you recommend?
- What do you think?

At first, they were surprised. Since I normally took over, this was the opposite of what they were expecting.

If they came up with an idea, I encouraged them to try it out. If they had no suggestions, I'd say, "Why don't you give it some thought, come up with some ideas and we can chat tomorrow? I have ten minutes at either 8:30 am or 4:15 pm." This was not easy for me at first. I found myself wanting to apologize. Sometimes, I'd shout out the door as they left, "But if you need me before then, just stop by, OK? You can knock even if the door is shut." ☺

It took me a while to be comfortable stepping into this type of leadership. I worried that I was coming off as uncaring or abrupt, but the opposite was happening. They felt trusted to make important decisions and were walking a little taller. Stepping out of my comfort zone had worked!

Next, I was able to move on and solve my next biggest productivity mistake: fear of delegation.

Productivity Mistake Number Four: Resisting Delegation

As I allowed others to begin solving their own problems, beginning to delegate became the next natural step. Delegation required that I trust them, and that wasn't easy. I had systems of my own, and I could do it fast, and just the way I liked it.

If you're not allowing others to do work, it's because you don't trust that they can do as quickly or as well as you can. This type of thinking is keeping you and your company hostage. When you don't allow people to learn the work, you're preventing them from becoming future leaders.

Holding people hostage and stunting their careers is not your intention, I know. It wasn't mine either. We want work to be done well. Some people take a long time to learn. Delegation requires patience. Sometimes it doesn't work the first few times. Sometimes we don't explain the process well. Sometimes we delegate to the wrong person. The key is to not give up.

Here is how I did it:

1. I gained the confidence to delegate when I realized the great results that were happening by allowing people to solve their own problems. Some of them began to ask for more responsibilities which made delegation easier the first few times. Those successes gave me the courage to offer additional projects to others.

2. Each week, I'd look at my project list and ask myself, "Which of these tasks need to be done by me and which can be done by someone else?" I began with a simple list on a legal pad. Tasks on one side, names of people across from them.

3. I then invited people for a chat. To prevent them from worrying, I told them right away what I wanted to talk about. Instead of saying to them, "Can you meet with me Friday at 1 pm, Mary?" I said, "Mary, as you know we have landed a new account and I'm in need of someone to handle the media contacts and publicity. I think you would be ideal for this. Are you available to discuss this on Friday at 1 pm?" This tactic eliminates surprise, reduces worry and allows them a few days to prepare

for the meeting.

4. Be sure to clearly communicate the end result. Let go of your need to control the process and trust them to come up with the best end result. They may surprise you with a better way.

5. At first, it's important to review progress before you get to that end result. You don't want to micro-manage, but you also want to be sure that they clearly understand what is expected.

6. Trust that the person will do an excellent job. Let them know that you feel confident in their abilities.

Delegation offers you the freedom to take on new projects, grow the business and receive promotions.[3] As you gain confidence in delegation, you'll get comfortable with the practice and begin to delegate at home or in your community service efforts. The young people that you influence, whether they are your own children or someone else's, also need practice to become independent leaders. Allow them to take on household chores and volunteer activities that help them to grow into responsible adults.

Productivity Mistake Number Five: Too Many Meetings

I don't have to tell you that you spend too much time in meetings. Today's innovative companies realize that meetings waste time and undermine effectiveness. Don't be afraid to be the first person to offer alternatives to meetings.

Let's assume that a department has a mandatory weekly meeting with five employees that lasts one hour. Shifting that to a 40-minute meeting instead saves a total of **100 minutes.** Shifting to a 30-minute meeting saves a total of **150 minutes** or 2 and a half hours of productivity regained.

Here is how to do it:

1. Suggest switching to 20, 30 or 40 minute time periods to increase productivity and eliminate overtime. If there is resistance, ask for a trial period of 30-60 days.

2. Distribute an agenda with a schedule in advance.

3. Begin on time, even if everyone has not arrived.

4. Begin by reminding attendees of the meeting's purpose and the stop time. Announce that you plan to stay on track with the agenda. There is no time today for complaints, social chatter, or "why this will never work" stories.

5. If the meeting gets derailed, some good phrases to use are: "We seem to be off track." or "Let's get back on topic."

6. End on time. If you have not accomplished everything on the agenda, make that the first priority of the next meeting.

7. Thank everyone for arriving on time, contributing and for their efforts to improve productivity.

Other ideas for more effective meetings:

- Change the name from "meeting" to "briefing"
- Try substituting 5 or 10-minute briefings for formerly 30-minute meetings
- Only include refreshments for celebrations
- When the meeting time is over, stand up and gather your things. This will encourage others to get back to their offices.

- For short meetings, remain standing. No need to sit down if you are having a briefing that is less than 10 minutes.
- Suggest a virtual check-in by phone or video chat to eliminate leaving the office
- Track your time savings and improvements
- Acknowledge others for making changes

It may take a few weeks to get everyone used to the new format. Remember that they are accustomed to long meetings and socializing before and after. Those habits are long-established and some folks won't be happy with a change. Don't give up. Change can be challenging but results like increased productivity, decreased work hours, effectiveness and momentum are worth the effort.

Productivity Mistake Number Six: Email Overwhelm

Email is one of the best time-saving tools available. When used correctly, it can leverage your time and increase your effectiveness. On the other hand, an out-of-control in-box with poorly managed email wastes time and drains productivity. I used to spend hours each day trying to keep on top of emails, rationalizing that I may miss something important. A few new smart habits changed that.

Here is how I did it:

1. **To-Do List Before Checking Email**
   I used to begin my day by making a cup of tea and checking email. There were days when responding to questions and requests took ninety minutes. Afterward, I needed a break to get ready to work. Frustrated with piles of work, I decided to focus my time on income producing activities and finishing the projects that were lacking attention. Just like the in-person interruptions,

the email questions began to solve themselves when I didn't give them immediate attention. This habit took a while to get used to but it was worth it. Now, the first thing I look at in the morning is my to-do list. I usually don't check email until after my first client or after my first two hours of doing productive work.

2. **Separate Work and Personal Email**
    Seeing an email from your bank or getting a notice about a sale at your favorite stores can be very distracting when trying to focus on work. This can also create a very cluttered inbox. With a separate account for your personal items you know just where to go when you need to find a receipt or a discount code for shopping. I use three emails:

-   One account for work
-   One account for finances and bill payments
-   One account for everything else

    Work email is much easier to organize when there is no excess clutter. This really helps to reduce distractions and procrastination.

3. **Goodbye Notifications**
    Alerts, sounds, and pop-ups are constant distractions that keep you from being focused. If you check email every few hours, you don't need distracting sounds and flashes calling your attention away from what you're working on. Find the settings in your email account and turn them off.

    If that makes you uneasy, set up special alerts for certain email addresses if you are waiting for an email from a VIP client, your boss or are expecting a media interview.

You'll be surprised at how reactive you've been and how much more intentional you can be without these thought interruptions. If you are active on any social media sites, I recommend that you adjust your account settings to receive ZERO email notifications. You may have to do a little digging to find these settings but this strategy eliminates a great deal of inbox clutter and removes the temptation to visit social media during the workday.

4. **More Intentional Work and Less Send/Receive**
   Many people have trained themselves to read emails the moment they arrive in the inbox. Email is a convenient communication tool but it's not meant for emergencies. Try switching your send/receive option to once per hour. Is there any real reason you need to check more often than that?

5. **Use Scheduled Emails**
   When you respond to emails instantly, you are training others to depend on you for an immediate response. Let's say a coworker sends you an email at 11 pm and you read it. If you reply at 11 pm, you've just set the precedent that you can be contacted at that time. Instead, reply to the email and use the "send later" option available from most email account providers. Schedule the response to go the next workday morning at 7:45 am. You appear competent and professional instead of reactive and always available.

These habits have allowed me to focus on important projects without distraction. I do not treat email as an intrusion in my day. In fact, I feel the opposite. It's a powerful tool and my favorite way to communicate right now.

Is your inbox stuffed? Check the resource section at the

back of this book to get a step by step guide and learn how I reduced my email in-box from tens of thousands to a few hundred in less than 30 days.

Commitment to Time Mastery

Remember:
Your example
(good or bad) of how to
manage yourself will
have an effect on
others, so be a great
time/life management
role model.

Like all Leadership Academy for Women graduates, you've just learned how to overcome the six biggest productivity drains on women today. The solutions did not include any:

- Strict Structures
- Military-Like Protocols
- Rigid Schedules
- Getting Up at 5 am
- Working Harder

Why? For good reason! Most women don't respond well to masculine productivity protocols. If you've been holding yourself to strict standards, I encourage you to STOP trying to adapt military-like rigidity into your life and work. Women are not designed to work that way but we've been trying to adapt to these styles since we entered the workforce. If you can let go of all of the "shoulds" that you think need to be a part of your routine and instead focus on living and leading intentionally, you may find that the natural feminine instincts that you were born with can be used to effectively accomplish everything that is needed.

[1] To learn how I stopped overbooking and overcommitting myself, go to **CoachBethCaldwell.com,** click on The Women Lead Movement and watch the video **6 Ways to say NO.**

[2] To watch my popular workshop **Empowered Productivity,** visit **CoachBethCaldwell.com** and click on The Women Lead Movement to find the recording.

[3] To watch my video with practical tips on delegation, go to **CoachBethCaldwell.com,** click on The Women Lead Movement and watch the video **The Power of Delegation.**

The difference between stumbling blocks and stepping stones is how you use them.

Chapter Two
Developing Emotional Resilience

The updated definition of resilience is to emotionally recover from adversity, illness, depression, or after having been bent, compressed or stretched to her extreme. I'm incredibly impressed by women who have experienced loss, disappointment, heartbreak, illness, unexpected change, trauma or other devastation and have gracefully rebuilt their lives even better than before. It seems that resilience comes naturally to some people, while others struggle and get stuck.

I've been able to bounce back from career challenges, serious illness, divorce, heartbreak, and financial ruin. However, a nasty comment made to me by a peer when I was age 17 damaged my confidence so much that I abandoned my dream of being a professional writer and speaker for most of the next twenty years.

Leadership Academy for Women students are given all the tools they need to become resilient and model emotional resilience to others.

When we foster emotional strength and health in ourselves and others, we become better able to cope with the difficulties and challenges of life.

Here is how I did it:

Emotional Resilience Strategy Number One: Feel Your Feelings

It's important that humans experience emotions. Feeling your feelings and processing emotions like grief, pain, disappointment and loss are important. Most people avoid these feelings but experiencing them is the first step toward developing healthy coping skills.

Research from Harvard trained neuroanatomist Dr. Jill Bolte Taylor shows that initial emotions last from 5-90 seconds. That is how long your body takes to process a feeling. According to her research, the worst emotion you can experience will last only 90 seconds.[1] People spend months, years and decades avoiding change or having awkward conversations, and when they finally face it, there are 90 seconds of discomfort. Then, change or healing begins.

Understanding this has helped me both personally and professionally. I noticed my tendency to resist negative emotions. When I did allow myself to feel disappointed, angry or sad, I discovered that the feelings or tears did not actually last long.

When working with a client that is processing something uncomfortable, I sit quietly and allow them to process. I don't feel awkward and I no longer rush to encourage or distract them. The brain and body do what is natural, experience the emotion and move on to the healing process.

Emotional Resilience Strategy Number Two: Discover Healthier Coping Skills

If you've avoided processing your feelings, you'll likely be participating in unhealthy or unproductive coping. How do you cope when you're not your best self?

Check all that apply:

- ☐ Work harder
- ☐ Withdraw
- ☐ Get irritable with those you care about most
- ☐ Sleep
- ☐ Obsessively clean
- ☐ Binge watch television
- ☐ Abuse food or alcohol
- ☐ Worry
- ☐ Avoid the person/s or situation that caused the conflict
- ☐ Constantly review the problem, alone in your head or to any friend who will listen
- ☐ _____
- ☐ _____
- ☐ _____

When it comes to changing any habit, the first step is awareness. When I have a client who is stuck, I often advise her to talk aloud to herself. A statement like this is powerful:

"Ever since (problem/situation/conflict) happened, I've been doing a lot of (enter your unhealthy coping choice here). That's interesting."

Saying "that's interesting" is neutral and helps to keep you from judging yourself.

Next, you'll probably want to say something like "Why do I always do this?" or "What's the matter with me?" Those questions don't lead to a solution and will keep you feeling down. It's better to pose a question that will lead to progress. Try something like this:

"Ever since (problem/situation/conflict) happened, I've been doing a lot of (enter your unhealthy coping choice here). That's interesting.

What is a more positive choice to help me feel better?"

You may think of an instant solution and you may not. The important thing is to change your thoughts toward seeking better coping habits. As soon as you ask the question, your amazing brain will begin seeking a solution.

There are two types of healthy coping skills, **emotional** and **practical**.

Some ideas to help you feel better **emotionally:**[2]
- Inspirational or happy music
- Long relaxing bath
- Aromatherapy
- Exercise
- Take a walk or experience nature
- Cook a favorite recipe
- Fun activities with family or friends
- Laugh
- Spend time with children
- Spend time with animals

When I notice that I'm engaged in unhealthy coping habits, I turn to music, laughter, and aromatherapy. They help me feel better immediately. I have a playlist of favorite uplifting motivational songs on YouTube and a board on Pinterest with my favorite funny videos.[3]

Sometimes your healthy coping skills will be practical action. Let's say that you received harsh criticism for a project at work. You are surprised, disappointed and embarrassed. After feeling and processing these feelings, choose some sensible **practical** actions.

You could try:

- Reviewing the project to determine how the miscommunication happened and what can be improved next time. 22

- Asking for clear and concise expectations on the next project.
- Request a mentor.
- Hire a coach to help you with communication or other skills.
- Take a class or read books to help you improve.
- Volunteer to take on a similar project to get more practice and show your improvement.

The next time you find yourself buffering your emotions and coping unproductively, give these healthier strategies a try.

Emotional Resilience Strategy Number Three: Proactive Health

I've noticed that when I'm feeling capable, confident and healthy I handle stress and disappointment much better than when I'm tired, overwhelmed and have been making poor food choices. I'm much more emotionally sensitive if I allowed myself to get overbooked, skipped my day of food prep, or said yes to more obligations than I can realistically handle. Understanding this about myself makes it easier for me to prioritize health and emotional well being. I had to replace my bad habits with new proactive tools to keep me physically and emotionally healthy.

Here is how I did it:
1. Dedicated family time every week. (Using my ideal schedule this is easy)
2. Pre-scheduled health appointments with my naturopath, chiropractor and Reiki/massage therapist.
3. Scheduled breaks that include time outdoors.
4. Electronic-free time before bed to ensure a good night of rest.
5. Scheduled time with my significant.
6. Social time with my friends.

7. Saying NO to things that don't make sense for me.
8. Delegating and accepting help.
9. Enjoying music.
10. Remembering to laugh every day.

Your list may be similar. It's important that you permit yourself to experience joy, fun, and healthy choices every day. Addressing your health when you're sick is reactive. Taking good care of yourself emotionally and physically every day is proactive.

Emotional Resilience Strategy Number Four: Positive Thoughts

Question: How many kind things have you thought about yourself since you got up this morning?

I can't help but notice when women use negative self-talk. Here are some of the comments that I've overheard recently:

- I feel silly asking this.
- People will think I'm lazy if I admit that I hired a housekeeper.
- I'm not exactly crushing it this month.
- I just got three new clients but they weren't as high paying as I hoped.
- I got no work done at all when I was on vacation.
- I only got about one-third of my to-do list completed.
- I wish I could produce as much as this one man in my office.
- I should get up earlier.
- Why do I have to be so chatty?
- I wish I had her style.
- I wish I could be more organized.
- I have ugly feet.

We're all guilty of talking like this to ourselves sometimes.

When you look at the statements above, can you imagine saying these things to your friends, colleagues or employees?

As with all other habits, awareness is the first step. My significant, Paul helped me with this in the funniest way. Once, when he heard me being critical of myself he said, "Hey, that's my girlfriend you're talking about!" That made me laugh out loud but it also made me realize that I needed to take my own advice.

When you catch yourself thinking or saying things that are unkind to yourself, pause and ask these questions:

Is that true?
Is that fair?
Is that relevant to any other woman in the same situation?
What is the truth?

Instead of This:	Say/Think This:
I feel silly asking this.	I have a question.
I'm not exactly crushing it.	My to-do list is a little nuts.
I've only done 1/3 of my list.	I got important tasks completed.
These clients aren't high-paying.	I just increased business by 150%.
I got no work done on vacation.	I spent quality time with my family.
I should get up earlier.	When I rest well I perform better.
I'd like to produce more/like a man.	I'm fortunate to enjoy flexibility.

25

I wish I had her style.	My style fits me.
I wish I could be more organized.	It's not like me to be scattered.
I have ugly feet.	My feet are good to me.
I'm embarrassed to have help.	I'm blessed to be able to afford help.

Here are some other common word/thought replacements:

Instead of:	Say/Think:
Failed	Attempted
Embarrassed	Surprised or Disappointed
Foolish	Took a risk
Unqualified	Competent
Not good enough	Better next time

Being kind to yourself is an important step in feeling secure, strong, and having pride in your accomplishments. When you feel good and then encounter a disappointment, receive bad news or criticism, you'll be able to cope in a more positive way.

Emotional Resilience Strategy Number Five: Cultivate Purpose

When I attended a personal development workshop many years ago, I was reminded that our life is not just about work and family. Even though that weekend was full of powerful and life-changing processes, there is one important exercise that remains with me today. It was the PIE of Life Exercise, now called the PIE of Prosperity®.

When the facilitators explained the importance of each piece of the Pie of Life, I immediately realized I had been neglecting most of what is needed to be an emotionally secure and healthy individual. All of my waking minutes were devoted to either working or caregiving. I was ignoring 75% of the pie.

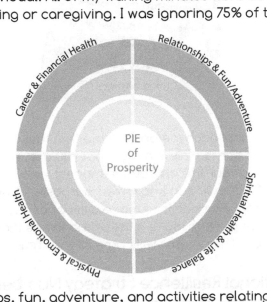

Relationships, fun, adventure, and activities relating to spiritual, physical, or emotional health were missing from my life. I hadn't enjoyed any of these for years. I had abandoned many of the experiences that used to bring joy and purpose to my life. We were not designed to work and serve 18 hours each day. What joys have you forgotten?[4]

I've learned that enjoying activities outside of work and family allows us to tap into a purpose. Having a purpose helps us feel connected, needed, and fulfilled. You are needed! Your gifts are important. Your ideas, energy, and efforts could be solving some of the world's problems RIGHT NOW.

I don't believe that we have just one purpose in life. I believe that we have many throughout our lives. A woman with purpose will be able to handle emotional challenges better than one who feels that her only role is to work and serve.

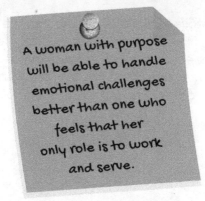

A woman with purpose will be able to handle emotional challenges better than one who feels that her only role is to work and serve.

Women often approach me and tell me that they have no idea what their purpose is. This is a sign that you are working too much and living your life in reactive mode. I've been there. The truth is that ONLY YOU can know your purpose. If you are stuck on this, a helpful exercise is to make a list of all the things you don't enjoy doing. Then make a list of the things that feed your soul. Then wait. The answer will come to you. Trust yourself.

Emotional Resilience Strategy Number Six: Awareness, Acceptance, and Appreciation

When my book **Smart Leadership** was published in 2014, I was able to travel around the United States meeting and working with companies who had leadership and employee challenges. I became known as a woman who wasn't afraid to tell the truth, address problems, and create solutions. Teams who had been frustrated with poor performance, personality conflicts and bad behavior sought out my solutions and advice. Some of the problems I encountered were shockingly unprofessional with a profound lack of social and emotional maturity.

I remember teaching a workshop to a community leadership group that included about sixty leaders from different industries in the region. They were especially upset with underperforming employees and were using the excuse, "You just can't hire good help in this town." I remember listening to them share their many frustrations and long list of bad behaviors being exhibited by their workforce. They were convinced that there was no hope. As they stared at me, expecting sympathy I simply said, "I just don't believe that every employee in this town is a useless asshole."

There were a few gasps and the room became silent. Knowing how long it takes to process emotions and new realizations, I stayed quiet, avoided the gaze of the shocked meeting planner and waited. It was about 5 seconds before the room burst into laughter.

Until now, these leaders believed that there was no solution available. They convinced themselves that the region offered nothing but under-performers and there was no hope. I explained to them what have now become my three fundamental principles of leadership:

1. Every individual has potential.
2. Most people are doing the best they can.
3. People will live up or down to the expectations that you set for them.

Now they realized that the solution was to become better leaders. Once you become aware of and admit the real problem, you can begin to seek solutions.

The next step for this group was acceptance. They had to accept that the leadership tools they were using were not working. They had to accept that humans come with a range of skill sets. It was time to stop being frustrated by expecting them to be different than they were, and instead, use their knowledge to create incentives and training that created future leaders.

Finally, I asked them to change their focus entirely and create an appreciation list. These folks had been griping for so long they had come to expect under-performance from everyone. I gave them five minutes to make a list. Five minutes of silence is a long time when you're in a group, but I knew this was important. They had spent many years focusing on negativity. This could not be a thirty-second exercise. Most took more than a minute to think of something. Some insisted there was nothing to write down. I gave them some prompts:

- Who comes to work on time every day?
- Who always smiles and is friendly?
- Is there someone who is always finding mistakes that need to be fixed? They are saving you money.
- Who tells all of their friends and family when there is a job opening at your plant?
- Who is the first to volunteer to stay late or fix something that isn't working?

When the time was up, I had them break into small groups and read their lists aloud. The appreciation became contagious. The lists began to spark ideas and memories. I was excited to see people adding even more to their lists. The energy in the room had changed from discouragement to optimism. The event planner smiled and clapped to me from across the room. She later told me that they had never had a speaker who'd been able to motivate this group. Appreciation is a powerful resource.

When you're not feeling your best, remember to allow awareness, acceptance, and appreciation into your thoughts. I encourage my clients and Leadership Academy students to set aside time for appreciation every day. When you focus on what is going well in your life and business, you're emotionally more resilient and will be able to shift from discouraged to inspired. Even better, you'll be a role model for others around you to do the same.

[1] Read more about Dr. Jill Bolte Taylor's research here: http://drjilltaylor.com/book.html

[2] For some practical strategies that will help you process emotions visit **CoachBethCaldwell.com** and watch the video titled **Stop Avoiding Your Emotions and Tell The TRUTH!**, or download the free ebook **Best Ways to Fix Your Funk.**

[3] Find the links to my playlists and things that make me laugh, at **CoachBethCaldwell.com**. Click on the tab that says **Women Lead Movement.**

[4] To take your own PIE of Prosperity® Mindset Self-Assessment, visit https://createathrivinglifestory.com, and click on assessments.

If you don't step forward, you'll
always be in the same place.

Chapter Three
Polish Your Professional Presence

The very first task that Leadership Academy students complete is a review and refresh of their personal brand. If you're not familiar with the term brand, it's your personal image combined with your professional presence. How you speak, sound and appear reflects not only on you but also on your company. We've learned In the past to improve how our image comes across in-person (offline), but today's leaders need to be aware of how they appear on the internet (online). During Leadership Academy, students work to improve their personal brands on both platforms.[1]

Here are the brand items the students review and improve:

1. **Voicemail Greeting**
   Imagine that a senior leader from your company calls to arrange a meeting with you about a promotion. Perhaps a potential new client or a news producer calls your number and listens to your voicemail greeting. What do they learn about you? Do they hear an automated message? Are you apologetic? I want them to hear your voice and think, "YES! Just what we're looking for!" Call yourself now and pay attention to how your greeting sounds.
   - Is your voice confident and clear?
   - Is there background noise?
   - Do you apologize for not being available?

- Do you include your name and title?

This is a piece of your brand that can be professionally polished in a few moments.

2. **Email Signature Line**
   Another very simple way to improve your professional presence is your email signature line. It should include your full name, title and contact information. Your photo or company logo is an additional option that will allow you to stand out from your colleagues and competition.[2]

3. **Professional Photo**
   Your headshot photo will be used for your company website, award applications, press releases, social media profiles, membership listings, and other marketing or promotional materials. Be sure that your photo is taken by a professional photographer, less than 3-5 years old, and portrays you in a professional manner.[3]

4. **Personal Bio**
   A bio (short biography) is a short overview that briefly highlights your accomplishments and work. Imagine it as what you'd read on the back cover of a book if you were the author. Women often resist having a

professional bio. That's why we pair students up in Leadership Academy. A bio is required for graduation and they find it easier to write each others' bios. They are printed and read aloud at graduation. There is something very empowering about seeing your professional bio in print, so don't avoid this. Update your bio often and add new certifications, awards, media features, promotions, etc. as they happen.

5. **Association, Membership and Volunteer Profiles**
   Once you have a quality professional headshot and bio, I recommend that you create a folder on your desktop so you can easily access this information whenever needed. Then, take the next step. Update the information on all of your association and membership profiles. I don't want someone to Google you and see a blank ghost face image and no words where your information should be. Use these memberships as a tool to leverage yourself. You never know what opportunities may arise or who may come across your information.

6. **Listing of Awards, Media Features and Recognition**
   If you've received awards and recognition for career accomplishments or work that you've done in the community, allow those credentials to be reflected within your bio, company website and on your social media profiles.

When you feel confident about your professional presence, you'll be more comfortable with the next strategy: Being the first one to speak up and address conflict.

[1] A helpful **Brand You Review Checklist** is included in the resource section of this book.

[2] You'll find sample voice message greetings and email

signatures to help you appear polished and professional included in the resource section of this book.

[3] Download a free copy of the ebook: **The Professional Woman's Guide to a Fantastic Professional Photo,** at CoachBethCaldwell.com. Click on the Women LEAD! Movement page.

It's absolutely appropriate to handle conflict without being aggressive.

Chapter Four

Confidence and Courage: Masculinity Not Required

One of the most popular classes in Leadership Academy for Women is called **Confident Communication.** This is usually taught in week four while the students are still getting to know one another. They are just beginning to share the conflicts happening in their workplaces and admitting how they avoid talking about or addressing the issues. Most fear appearing aggressive, being called a bitch, or making the situation worse.

During the course, the students learn communication and conflict strategies that aren't aggressive or confrontational. The women agree to go back to the office and try one of the new approaches. For the next several weeks we spend the first fifteen minutes of class enjoying their success stories. We hear how they have been able to influence change without being aggressive or experiencing negative side effects. Each week their confidence grows and they inspire each other to step out of their comfort zones a little more. You can do the same.

Here is how to get started:

Confidence and Courage Strategy Number One: Speak Up

Speaking up has never been a problem for me. When a

39

company hires me as a consultant to deal with long-term issues and big problems, they appreciate the fact that I speak up and tell the truth immediately. I simply say what I see.

I once worked with a company that had over 300 employees in their research division. One section within this division was having a huge problem. They had one cranky employee who was causing a significant disruption. I'll call him Frank. No one wanted to work with Frank because, well, Frank didn't work. He hadn't always been a troublesome employee. In fact, his performance reviews from the first twelve years of employment were all satisfactory. I learned that he became defiant and troublesome when computers were integrated into his division. When that happened, Frank told his supervisors that he did not work on "those machines." His supervisor at the time, a young female, was intimidated by his aggressive manner. She coped with the situation by assigning his work to other staff members and picking up the slack herself. She tried enrolling Frank into computer training programs but he never completed the coursework.

Eventually, she transferred to another department and a new supervisor inherited Frank. This happened several times. No one wanted to deal with Frank's moodiness. Co-workers continued to pick up the slack. Frank did very little work and spent most of his workday socializing with fellow employees, having coffee and doing crossword puzzles. He was sent to computer training several times but never completed any courses. Years went by. Now newer and younger employees were less tolerant of cranky behavior and doing work that they weren't being paid for. They chose to leave for a different department or a different company.

The newest supervisor, an ambitious and solution-driven mid-thirties man named Dan, was determined to solve this problem when he contacted me. I met with a small group to discuss the situation in their conference room. "Frank's last supervisor told me that the consensus was to ignore the issue. Frank has only six years before retirement. Honestly, I don't want to wait this out. We are losing too many talented people because of this."

I was surprised that a company this large would tolerate this type of dysfunction for any amount of time. "How long have you been having this problem?" I asked. The Human Resources Representative replied immediately. "Twelve years," she stated without emotion. I was really surprised. The feeling in the room was awkward while I processed this information. The lawyers looked at their feet uncomfortably. Dan leaned toward me and asked, "Can you help?" A meeting was set for the following week.

I have to admit that I was a little nervous going into a room with Frank, especially after having read several reports and complaints about him. I had nothing prepared in advance and had no idea what to expect. The meeting consisted of his supervisor Dan, two staff attorneys, and two human resource professionals. Frank entered and everyone was tense. In his late 50's, he was dressed in old black work pants and a white undershirt, not the typical attire for the research department. His hair was slicked back and his chest was puffed out. I smiled and introduced myself. I explained that the reason I was here was to try and sort out the problem of frequent turnover. We were seeking solutions to help the department be more enjoyable and less stressful. I had to resist the urge to smile when Frank said to me, "People just don't want to work these days, that's why they keep leaving. They just don't want to work."

"Tell me about your workday, Frank." I smiled warmly. Frank stammered a little and said a few things. I let him know that I'd been reading through his file and noticed that for the first twelve years of his career he'd been happy at work and received positive performance reviews. "I can't help but notice, Frank, that all of your conflict began when research became computerized. I get the impression that you don't like

41

working with computers."

My tone was polite, but one of the human resource leaders gasped a little at my comment and one of the attorneys coughed uncomfortably. The room became more tense. Frank didn't seem to notice. "That is the absolute truth.", he said, his voice rising. "I told them from day one, I don't do computers." "Before that, did you enjoy your work?" I asked. "Oh, I did. I really did." was his reply.

I continued, "What did you enjoy?" followed by, "Do you enjoy your days now?" As he answered, I looked him in the eye and nodded along. It was fascinating to watch him talk about the early days and how he enjoyed work. His voice had lowered and he did not seem as agitated.

"I have a question," I said, now addressing the entire room, "Has anyone ever tried to find another place for Frank within the company? Are there any jobs where he can work for the next six years where he doesn't have to use a computer?"

I then turned back to Frank and looked him in the eye. "I'm sure you understand that the company cannot keep paying you for work that you are not doing. Have you ever thought about working in a different department?" He immediately replied, sitting straight up in his chair. "You know I have thought a few times that maybe I could work in security. They work shifts and weekend hours and don't use computers. My wife and I enjoy fishing and camping. If I worked in security, we could go away during the week like the other guys do."

I turned to human resources. "Are there any openings in security?" They said nothing but nodded yes. I looked directly at the employment law attorneys. "Do you see any issues in transferring Frank?" They shook their heads no. I turned back to Frank. "Frank, if there is any training required for this new job, can I count on you to attend enthusiastically and complete the coursework?" "YES MA'AM, YES INDEED," he smiled. "I cannot wait to tell my wife. She is going to be so happy to hear this."

Frank nearly skipped out of the room. The group was quiet for a few minutes. Eventually, one of the human resource professionals said, "I've been working here for twenty years and I've never seen that man smile."

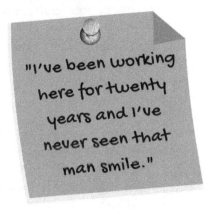

I looked at my watch. The meeting had lasted fifteen minutes. A problem that went on for twelve years was solved because someone had the courage to tell the truth.

"You don't like working with computers."

It was a simple fact and it was said without judgment. No emotion, no drama, no frustration, no anger, no yelling, no fighting. When you encounter conflict, gather your courage and speak the truth. There may be awkward moments or uncomfortable feelings but telling the truth is the crucial first step toward a solution.

Confidence and Courage Strategy Number Two: Face Awkward Conversations With Confident Responses

How many times have you been confronted with an awkward

situation and found yourself speechless? Hours, even days later, you finally come up with a brilliant reply.

I've discovered that the reason we don't handle uncomfortable situations well is because we're surprised and unprepared for them. Usually, the person who has you in the space of discomfort is doing or saying something you would never think of doing. Therefore, you have no response.

Over the years I've created a collection of go-to responses for awkward conversations.

Here they are:

1. For the dinner party or networking guest that won't stop talking, say this: *I don't want to monopolize your time. I've enjoyed meeting you, Susan. I wish you the best with that knee replacement.* (smile and turn away)

2. For the person who is trying to sabotage or compete with another employee by spreading lies about them, say this: *I disagree. I've always found John to be very professional.* Or, *I've never worked with Amy. I'll wait to get to know her before forming an opinion.*

3. For the person who has a strong political opinion and assumes that everyone else agrees with them, say this: *That's an interesting perspective.* (smile and turn away)

4. For the person who is now trying to get you to agree with their opinion even though you don't want to engage, say this:
I don't agree, but you have given me something to think about. (smile and walk away)

5. When the person who has a strong opinion is not getting the message that you don't want to engage with

them and keeps telling you more about what they think, trying to sway you to their side, say this: *This is obviously very important to you, Jim. I don't engage in political debates at work. Speaking of work, we both should get back to it.* (smile and turn away)

There is no reason for you to ever spend another moment of your life engaged in conversation that drains your energy and keeps you from work or family.[1] If all else fails, you can try this statement: Fascinating. Excuse me.

Confidence and Courage Strategy Number Three: Planning and Preparing for Conflict Conversations

As you continue to be promoted at work or add employees to your business, you'll have the opportunity to practice handling more conflict. I think you've learned by now that it's best to address issues by facing the truth. The women who begin at Leadership Academy are usually not comfortable navigating conflict but when they learn this system, they are willing to give it a try. When they realize that these issues are not as difficult to solve as they once feared, they begin dealing with issues immediately.

Her e is the system that they learn:

1. Before scheduling a meeting to discuss a problem, **first assess the situation** and determine an acceptable outcome. What is the best solution? What will work for all parties involved? Type this out in large font and keep it in your notebook during the meeting. Refer to it as needed.

2. Invite all parties to the meeting and **let them prepare in advance** by announcing the topic that is going to be discussed. This alleviates the fear of the unknown and allows them to think about the situation ahead of time. Otherwise, they may be surprised and unprepared to discuss the topic. They may even need time to think, requiring another meeting.

3. When you send a meeting announcement, **be specific about the duration** of the meeting. Let them know that you plan to be prompt with start and stop times.

4. **Think about each participant** that will be attending or involved. What motivates them? What are they most afraid of? Thinking about this in advance allows you to be prepared with some answers and suggestions.

5. Begin on time and **remind everyone of the stop time.** "We have 20 minutes before my conference call, so let's keep on topic."

6. Your first statement should **be reassuring.** "No one is losing their job today." or "I've been giving this a lot of thought and I feel confident that we can solve this problem." Understand that if everyone is worried about a negative outcome, they won't be fully listening to you. Reassuring everyone from the beginning allows them to relax and participate fully.

7. Next, **state the obvious.** "As you are all aware, we have a problem." Name the problem and the ideal outcome. If appropriate ask for ideas and feedback. Designate a timeline. Assign a person to track progress. Schedule a follow-up meeting if necessary.

8. **End on time.** Stand up when the meeting is complete. Thank everyone for their efforts. Let them know that you genuinely appreciate that this was not an easy situation to face. Follow up privately with individual thank you's and encouragement.

Hopefully, as you've been reading this, you've imagined yourself leading such a meeting.[1] Have you thought of issues and conflicts from the past that you wish were handled like this?

Confidence and Courage Strategy Number Four: Remove Minimizers and Apologies from Your Thoughts, Words, and Writing

- This is a silly question.
- I'm so scattered, I forgot.
- I'm not sure if this is a good suggestion.
- Does that make sense?
- I'm not an expert, but...
- I just need a minute of your time.
- I'm sorry, that's not what I ordered.
- I'm sorry, I cannot volunteer for the fundraiser.
- I'm sorry I'm crying.

This is probably not the first time you've read that women apologize far too often. We seem to have a habit of minimizing ourselves with words and phrases such as sorry, just, actually, I'm no expert, etc.

Fortunately, women are becoming more aware of these

tendencies. Popular social sharing of videos[2] on this topic help with awareness. New interactive apps like Grammarly are being developed to warn us about the tone of our written words.[3]

As you become more aware of how often you minimize and apologize, you can begin to replace these habits. Here are some suggestions:

Instead of:
I just need a minute of your time.

Say this:
I have that report ready.

Instead of:
This is a silly question.

Say this:
I have a question.

Instead of:
I'm so scattered, I forgot.

Say this:
I'll have that ready tomorrow.

Instead of:
I'm not sure if this is a good suggestion.

Say this:
Here's a suggestion.

Instead of:
Does that make sense?

Say this:
What are your questions?

Instead of:
I'm sorry, that's not what I ordered.

Say this:
There has been a mistake. I ordered____.

Instead of:
I'm sorry, I cannot volunteer for the fundraiser.[4]

Say this:
It's not possible for me to help this year. I hope you have a successful event.

Instead of:
I'm sorry for crying.

Say this:
Thanks for understanding.

Women have unique gifts that allow them to be effective and influential leaders. It's time to trust your intuition, tap into your empathy, state the obvious, stop apologizing and lead your team to a more productive and effective future.

[1] Download a tip sheet with reminders about the strategies you've learned to avoid awkward conversations and handle conflict at **CoachBethCaldwell.com,** click on the **Women Lead Movement.**

[2] Watch my favorite videos about women who apologize at the Women Lead Movement webpage, mentioned above.

[3] You can sign up for Grammarly for free here: https://app. grammarly.com/.

[4] Get a link to one of my most popular workshops, **Six Ways to Say No and Still be Nice** at the Women Lead Movement webpage, mentioned above.

Women have the inside edge on empathy, a negotiation super-power.

Chapter Five
Dedicated to Diplomacy:
Use Your Feminine Skills to Negotiate

Whenever I'm invited to teach a workshop on negotiation, the room is always filled with a diverse range of women. They register right away, show up early and stay late. Women seem to be fascinated with the subject. I've presented this topic to many hundreds of women, some of them attending multiple classes. Sadly, very few of them muster the courage to practice what they have learned.

I always ask the audience: Why do you avoid negotiation? Their answers include:

- Lack of confidence
- Conflict avoidance
- Assume a topic or offer is not open to negotiation
- Fear of being labeled as pushy, selfish, or aggressive

My next question: What do you think you're giving up when you avoid negotiating?

Their answer: silence in the room while they fail to meet my gaze until finally, one person hollers out, "saving money or getting a raise!"

YES, and so much more. Here is what you risk losing when you don't ask or negotiate:

- Salary increase
- Paid education
- Better title
- Improved benefits
- Fair workload
- Equal representation

Just saying the word negotiation can be intimidating. My first awareness of the word was hearing about hostage negotiations on the news when I was very young. No wonder some of us find the word frightening. The first thing I teach my students is to consider the positive aspects of negotiation. Instead of fearing what you may lose, think about all there is to gain.

Women's inherent skills make them excellent negotiators. Have you ever:
- Mediated a disagreement between a group of elementary school children?
- Convinced a toddler to wear their socks?
- Come to an agreement with a teenager on a curfew?
- Created a plan with a doctor, lawyer or administrator on behalf of a loved one?
- Advocated for a school, church or community organization that you cared about?

Chances are, you tapped into your natural gifts of empathy, tolerance, and compassion to create a desirable outcome. Women normally don't see a situation as black and white. They don't normally compartmentalize people and situations or separate them. Usually, women are able to empathize, understand and resolve situations easily by using their natural gifts.

I used to avoid negotiation, along will all other forms of confrontation. Now, I get paid to negotiate.

Here is how I did it:

1. I internally renamed negotiation to "creative problem solving". I learned this from an early mentor. Doing so helped me feel enthusiasm and confidence instead of fear about the process.

2. I planned ahead and wrote down what I wanted to gain during the negotiation and what I was willing to give up. In the early days, I flipped open my portfolio and reviewed my notes constantly.

3. I'd directly ask the person, "What do you not want to give up and why?" This helped me understand what they feared. Knowing this upfront often shortens discussion time and helps to avoid conflict.

Here's how you can do it too:

1. Focus on common goals and seek win/win outcomes instead of win/lose.

2. Stay fully present at all times, listening carefully to others and asking questions for clarification to avoid misunderstandings.

3. Remain focused on the end result.

4. Keep to the topic at hand. Example: "I appreciate that this is difficult. Regardless of your feelings, Bob, these budget cuts are happening and we are making the decisions today."

5. Show empathy to all parties (including yourself).

It's helpful to prepare yourself emotionally before having a negotiation conversation. Once you have decided what you hope to achieve, your must-haves and what you're willing to give up, think about this:

- What sets you off or triggers an emotional response from you?
- How will you stay calm?
- What's your plan if you become emotional?

Just because you don't intend to get aggressive or nasty doesn't mean your opponent won't. Know what sets you off. When I first began negotiating, it was pretty easy to get me off-topic or upset. A good bully will be able to quickly determine just what can set a person off and trigger an emotional response. Derailing a meeting by throwing others off emotionally is a tactic that some people use to give them an edge. Don't fall for that.

For example, in the past, if an opponent belittled me, accused me of cheating, or told a lie about me, I'd get upset and have to ask for a break to compose myself. If that were to happen today, I'd simply say, "That's not true." I no longer feel defensive or emotional. This old tactic no longer throws me off. In fact, the more confident I've become, the less often bullies have tried to rattle me.

Final tips for negotiation:

- It's not helpful to negotiate in an emotional state. Ask for and offer a break when needed.

- Be curious. Ask questions for clarification.

- Re-state and ask, am I understanding this?

- Be aware that what is said isn't always what is heard.

- Remember that you can't change people, you can only influence them.

- Don't attack people, attack issues.

- Attempt WIN/WIN outcomes as often as possible.

- Don't schedule other meetings on the day of a negotiation. Take the time you need to prepare beforehand. Allow time to rest emotionally afterward.

- Thank all parties for participating, regardless of the outcome.

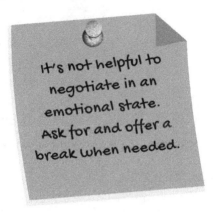

It's not helpful to negotiate in an emotional state. Ask for and offer a break when needed.

I hope you've discovered that negotiations can be handled in a calm, competent and confident manner. There is never a need for bullying, insulting, intimidating or reducing anyone to tears.

Don't wait any longer! Begin now to use your natural gifts to negotiate effectively. Soon you'll be inspiring other women to do the same.

Just because it's always been done that way doesn't mean that's the way it should happen.

Chapter Six

Using Positive Expectations to Improve the Workplace

American workplaces have a great deal of room for improvement. The evidence is staggering. A recent **State of The Workplace** poll offered by Gallup reports that 33% of American workers are engaged at work compared to 70% of workers at the best organizations.[1] A separate and independent Yoh/Harris Poll recently revealed more disappointing information about the status of discontent in the workplace.[2]

The most common employee complaints about management include:

- Micromanaging
- Broken promises
- Unrealistic expectations
- Harsh criticism
- Lack of respect
- Not listening to or valuing employee opinions
- Managers with limited job knowledge

The poll also reveals that women today are more likely to consider alternative job offers than they had in previous decades.

Innovative, successful, positive workplaces have shaken

up the conventional workforce. They prove that happy and vibrant atmospheres can improve profitability. The old attitudes, "we've always done it this way" and "that's the way it is, don't expect change" are not being tolerated as they once were. Online forums now allow employees to anonymously report bad management behaviors, warning potential new talent to stay away. Companies that have primarily focused on profits and not bothered to improve working conditions now struggle to remain competitive. Employees don't feel loyal anymore. They leave bad workplaces for better pay and more positive working conditions.

At Leadership Academy, we spend a lot of time discussing workplace culture and how to improve it. What kind of workplace environment do you picture when you think about these companies?

- Apple
- Google
- Southwest Airlines
- Delta Airlines
- Spirit Airlines
- Walmart
- Nordstrom
- Tiffany & Co.
- Nabisco
- Fox News
- Lifetime Television
- Chick-fil-A
- United Way
- Internal Revenue Service
- Social Security Administration

Which of the companies above strike you as a great place to work? Which don't seem as desirable?

What do you admire about the workplaces listed above?

What do you think is lacking?

How does your current company compare?

Aside from those detailed in the Yoh/Harris Poll, other common employee complaints include:

- Inept management
- Immature behavior
- Miscommunication
- Gossip
- Drama
- Competitiveness
- Bullying

Our country spent 83 billion dollars[3] on training and leadership development last year, yet we're still overwhelmed with dissatisfaction in the workplace. What is missing?

During my **Smart Leadership** book tour, this topic was on my mind a lot. I was able to meet and work with a variety of leaders and discuss their biggest problems. When I compared the workplace culture of the most successful companies to those who struggle with poor performance, I discovered that improving culture in the workplace comes down to two simple tactics:

1. Successful companies offer clear expectations and address issues immediately. They share company goals and keep employees informed of status. Senior leadership is intentional, engaged and acts as a part of the team.

2. Companies that struggle don't define or explain the expectations of managers or staff. They spend most of their time in reactive mode, bouncing from one drama to another. There are no specific goals. Plans are shared with senior managers only. Bad behavior is

either tolerated or ignored.

It comes down to EXPECTATIONS and TOLERATIONS.

This is what the Leadership Academy for Women students focus on. First, they clearly define the roles of every individual on the team (expectations) and, instead of ignoring the problem, they take fast action when team members are unhappy or unproductive (tolerations).

When people don't know what's expected of them, they usually don't make amazing progress or achieve stellar results.

It's the company's role to have clearly defined expectations regarding branding, positioning, products, customer service, community involvement, ethics and integrity. This includes every detail about how the company is to be run and the expectations and role of each team member. A lot of companies skip this, but the ones who are successful and thriving are great at communicating expectations.

When is the last time you reviewed your expectations regarding workplace culture? If you've never done this, or haven't for a long time, you're not alone. Many companies and organizations score poorly when communicating their mission and the roles of employees. When people don't know what's expected of them, they usually don't make amazing progress or achieve stellar results.

If you are squirming uncomfortably right now, here's some good news: You can re-examine and improve expectations and tolerations at any time.

If this has never happened, know that you cannot just write out expectations and distribute them via a company memo or add this to your website.

As much as we'd like to write up new expectations and have everyone accept them with enthusiasm, an implementation process should be planned. Resist the natural urge to push this task off to human resources. Changes and policies should be handled by senior leaders. People feel most comfortable being led by someone who knows exactly where they are going.

Not everyone will be eager to embrace change.
Some people have enjoyed getting paid for doing no work.

Once expectations have been clearly communicated, you should see an immediate uptick in performance, retention and results. Be aware that not everyone will be eager to embrace change. Some employees have been enjoying underperforming and getting paid for it. They may not be as enthusiastic. Don't be like Frank's supervisor. When an employee is underperforming or sabotaging success, re-communicate expectations. Be curious, ask questions, and take action if things don't improve quickly. It may take some time but getting everyone motivated and on the same page is worthwhile and won't cost anywhere near 83 billion dollars.

If companies are to retain top talent and remain competitive, it is essential to create a workplace where expectations and tolerations are clearly communicated and maintained. Women leaders today are ideally positioned to influence and improve this situation. Are you ready to take it on?

[1] State of the American Workplace Report Gallup 2017

[2] Read the results of the Yoh/Harris Poll here: https://www.yoh. com/press-room/yoh-survey-top-issues-with-managers-that-would-make-employed-americans-consider-new-jobs.

[3] statista.com/statistics/788521/training-expenditures-united-states/

Multi-tasking is a female superpower. Remember to save those powers for when you're in danger.

Chapter Seven

Curating Calm

I have to admit that when I was first introduced to the practices of mindfulness and single-tasking, I was not enthusiastic. I had built a successful business using my skills as an extreme multi-tasker. I was comfortable doing several things at one time and had become accustomed to living and working in chaos. Still, I am always open to learning new things and my friends were adamant about getting me to meditate. As my friend Elaine put it, "Slow the f*ck down."

She dragged me to a Sunday morning meditation course on a farm about an hour outside of the city. As I was leaving, my ten-year-old niece warned me, "You know they are going to make you be quiet, right?"

To look the part, I wore boots and hiking clothes. As we entered the farmhouse, I was both nervous and curious. There were about 12 other students that day. After some introductions, the instructors began. I learned that while multi-tasking does have its perks it can lead to some dangerous side effects. I was already experiencing many of them.

The side effects of a high-paced, overbooked, chronic multi-tasking schedule include:

- Mental and emotional exhaustion
- Increased stress
- Elevated cortisol
- Memory loss
- Sleep disturbance
- Decreased productivity

The facilitators were enthusiastic about the perks that came along with what they were teaching. They insisted that if I slowed down, drank pure water, ate more whole foods and began to meditate 30 minutes every day, I'd be much happier. I didn't take all of their advice but I did feel calm after the workshop. I did some more research on the topic and began to incorporate some of what I was learning. About a year later, I added a 2-hour mindfulness course to the curriculum of Leadership Academy for Women. Yes, I found that slowing myself down helped me to become more efficient and effective. I felt more focused, more intentional and less scattered.

Curate some calm in your life by slowing down your busy mind.

At first, I began single-tasking with things like writing an article, crafting a proposal or calling a client. It didn't take long for me to enjoy the unfamiliar feelings of clarity and calmness. Single-tasking became easier for me. Calling a client while driving or in an airport terminal used to seem natural to me. Now it seemed counterproductive.

Do you constantly multi-task, feel frantic, or live and work in chaos? You may want to curate some calm in your life by slowing down your busy mind.

Here is how I did it:

Curating Calm Strategy Number One: Single-Tasking Instead of Multi-Tasking

1. My workday is separated into two-hour increments with breaks in between. I assign projects to each time block. Knowing that I have a limited amount of time to finish a task helps me to focus.

2. Since ideas constantly pop into my head, I have a pad and pen nearby to write down ideas. This keeps the momentum and I don't have to worry about forgetting something that occurred to me.

3. I don't have my phone near me and the ringer is off.

4. If needed, I use a "do not disturb" sign on the door.

5. All pop-up notifications on my computer have been disabled.

6. I shut down email and social media sites so the only thing in front of me is my current project.[1]

If you're like me, the natural desire to multi-task is very strong. Be kind to yourself as you try out these new habits. You've been multi-tasking for a very long time. I don't believe you have to give this habit up entirely. I still watch TV while I'm cleaning, listen to podcasts while I'm driving and I carry the trash downstairs along with the dirty laundry.

Curating Calm Strategy Number Two: Recognize the Signs of Stress, Burnout and Overwhelm Before You Blow

Have you ever:
Suddenly burst into tears?
Lost your temper or let someone push your buttons?
Overreacted to a situation?
Yelled at someone in traffic?

For most people, these extreme emotional reactions don't happen often. The truth is they don't have to happen at all.

With a good self-care plan and the awareness to recognize warning signs of emotional stress, you can prevent outbursts and the embarrassing repair work that has to be done afterward.

Think about the last time you overreacted. Were there any warning signs or signals that you missed? Your body sends messages to warn that you're reaching overwhelm. Every individual is different.

During times of extreme stress some symptoms I experienced were:

- I walked and talked very fast.
- I felt exhausted, even if I had slept for 8 hours.
- I was irritable and short-tempered.
- While driving, I noticed that I was clenching my teeth.

What are your symptoms? Here are some very common signs of emotional overwhelm. Check off the ones that seem familiar to you:

☐ Lack of energy
☐ Fuzzy brain, difficulty concentrating
☐ Feeling anxious
☐ Change in appetite
☐ Irritability
☐ Sleep issues
☐ Buffering--distracting yourself with binge TV, shopping, cleaning, alcohol/drug use, etc.
☐ Crying frequently or quick to anger
☐ Easily distracted
☐ Decrease in productivity despite being very busy

Families today are frantically busy. Even if they are unhappy, they stay that way because we all think this is normal. Trust me, I learned the hard way that when the body is telling you that you're over-stressing it, you should slow down. If you don't pay attention to them, the messages will become louder and louder until changes are made.[2]

A lot of women worry that if they slow down they will be less productive. I have found that the opposite is true for me personally, as well as for my students and clients. Our work is more thorough and complete. We feel calmer, healthier, happier, and more productive.

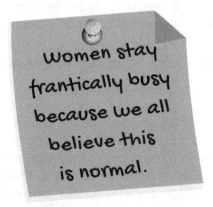

Women stay frantically busy because we all believe this is normal.

There are no more over-reactions, temper flare-ups or

emotional outbursts because we're no longer near burnout. We're not even close. Exhaustion, depletion, burnout and overwhelm are no longer words we use to describe ourselves, our schedules or our families.

What can you do to reduce emotional stress?

Here are some ways to start:

- Reduce the demands that you're placing on yourself [3]
- Prioritize wellness
- Ask for help from a friend, pastor, therapist or coach

Some of these habits have been with you for a lifetime, so it will take a while to change. When you find yourself becoming overwhelmed again, hopefully, you will recognize the signs early and make adjustments. If you are like me, you'll get lots of opportunities to practice. ☺

Once you become good at recognizing the signs of emotional stress and overwhelm in yourself, you'll also begin to notice these signs in others. By week ten, Leadership Academy students are already leaders in self-care. They have now begun to encourage colleagues to take better emotional care of themselves as well. This is an important and wonderful concept to share. Will you try it out and pass it on?

Curating Calm Strategy Number Three: Curiosity

Curiosity is a wonderful principle of mindfulness that encourages questions instead of judgment. We tend to immediately make judgments about people and situations based on our own experiences and fears. The next time you make a snap judgment, get curious and ask a question instead. This mindfulness principle will shake up the way you look at the world.

70

Here are some curiosity-instead-of-judgment examples:

Judgment: It's early spring and a neighbor's new dog is barking constantly. You decide, "My summer is now ruined. She obviously does not intend to care for this animal."

Curiosity: Your neighbor Norma's dog has been barking for hours. That's unusual. You check on your neighbor and learn that she forgot to put in her hearing aid. She's apologetic and feels awful for interrupting your day.

Judgment: Co-worker Robert has been irritable since you received a promotion. He didn't even apply for the position. He did congratulate you and seemed supportive. Since around that time he's become moody and unfriendly. He's often late, takes long breaks and never goes out for cocktails after work on Thursdays anymore. Obviously, he resents having to report to a woman.

Curiosity: Robert has always been supportive and friendly. You decide to ask him directly if there is an issue that has created conflict between the two of you. He apologizes and admits that he's become a full-time caregiver for his mother who has Alzheimer's Disease. He wasn't aware that his demeanor had changed and thought the stress had not affected him at work.

How much frustration have you caused for yourself by judging and assuming the worst about situations? Curiosity is a simple strategy that is easy to implement. Pairing curiosity with empathy can make a lasting impact on the way you lead, influence and support others.

Curating Calm Strategy Number Four:
Let it Go!

Resentment and anger are common enemies of a peaceful mind. It's natural for us to replay hurtful memories over and over again. I've been told that remembering the things that hurt us is the brain's way of keeping us safe. If we've been bitten by a rattlesnake and nearly died, we're supposed to remember that experience so that the next time we see a rattlesnake we run the other direction. The memory protects us from being harmed.

Are there past hurts and experiences that you keep reliving?

If so, ask yourself these questions:

1. Are those memories keeping me from harm or are they preventing me from moving on?
2. Is there a way that I can remember the lesson and let go of the painful feelings attached to the memory?

For many of us, replaying these experiences over and over again keeps us stuck. I recently received an urgent call from a financial services firm. Most of their managers have attended Leadership Academy. One of them, a financial services supervisor named Emily had recently been caught up in an ugly argument with a co-worker named Jacqueline. Emily was having a very hard time recovering emotionally. She was requesting to be allowed to work from home permanently. She had missed eleven days of work since the incident and insisted that she could no longer be in the same room as Jacqueline. The owners really valued Emily and wanted to keep her in the office. Working from home was not an option because of the required security in their industry. They asked if I could help.

I knew Emily to be emotionally mature and dedicated to her career. A few days later, we were sitting across from one another in a small conference room at the company headquarters. "So, what happened?" I asked gently. Emily talked for a while, describing her co-worker's immaturity and detailing every irritating moment of the weeks prior to the incident. She kept repeating, "I know she didn't mean it, I know she is going through a rough time, but I'm so upset about the things she said! I cannot stop hearing the words!" "Tell me the words," I said. I wrote down every ugly word as she repeated them. Some of them brought tears to my eyes. To make matters worse, this ugly outburst occurred in the lunchroom and was witnessed by several employees. Even though Emily was the victim, she felt embarrassed.

Emily broke down and began to sob. Knowing that this would pass in about thirty seconds, I stayed quiet while she finally felt those emotions. After she wiped her eyes and caught her breath, I showed her the list and asked, "Which of these statements are true?" She read each word carefully, tears welling up in her eyes again. "Absolutely none," she said quietly. I noticed that she sat up a little taller. She then showed me a letter written to her by Jacqueline the day after the incident. Jacqueline had written that she deeply regretted what happened and that she didn't mean the words she said. She was, as a condition to remain employed, seeking help from a counselor.

"I do actually forgive her," said Emily, " but I keep hearing those words over and over again."

"Do you think that returning to work may help?" I asked. She thought it would. We decided to create a plan to remove these hurtful thoughts. If we had been at one of my mountain retreats at that moment, I would have had her burn that paper in the fireplace. Since that was not possible in the office, we reviewed the list again. This time there were no tears. We agreed that nothing on the list was true or relevant. I walked down the hall with her and watched as she put the paper filled with hateful words in the shredder.

"I really feel a lot better." she said. "I'm worried, though, about the ride home. I have a 45-minute drive and when I get in the car, I just think about it over and over again." I asked if she had any favorite songs or playlists that had songs that made her feel happy, strong or proud. She remembered that suggestion from Leadership Academy and promised to make a playlist that weekend.

"WAIT!", she exclaimed. "I have the soundtrack to **Frozen** in my car. You know, that Disney movie? It's my daughter's favorite!" I nearly laughed out loud. I was familiar with the soundtrack. I sent Emily home with instructions to play the song "Let It Go" over and over until she could drive without thinking about it. Emily remembers that afternoon drive as one of the most enjoyable ones in her adult life. She later told me, "I screamed that song at the top of my lungs for almost an hour! When I got home I was in such a great mood!"

Happy and empowering music can help almost any situation but if you've experienced an emotional trauma, it's important that you ask for and be willing to accept help. I was once told that when we continue to remember and relive painful emotional experiences, it's the same as holding a hot coal against your heart and intentionally hurting yourself over and over again.

If you're doing this, here are some tools that have helped me:

- Reiki Treatments
- Qigong Classes
- Aromatherapy[4]
- Flower Essences
- Emotional Freedom Technique
- Traditional Therapy
- Writing or Being Creative
- Time in Nature
- Crying
- Time Alone
- Quality Sleep, Water and Nutrition
- Gratitude
- Forgiveness
- Acceptance

You will discover the methods that work best for you.[5] Recognize that emotional recovery takes time and you are doing your best.

Remember that you are a role model regardless of your title. People at work, at home and in the community will notice when you handle challenges with emotional maturity. When you keep your mind calm, avoid judgments, remain curious and let go of hard feelings, you're modeling intelligent behaviors that teach others to do the same.

[1] The Self-Control App is a great tool that allows you to block access to online websites that can distract you. Visit SelfControlApp.com.

[2] To read about how I recovered after overworking myself into a serious illness, pick up a copy of the book **From Frantic to Focused: How to Shift from Out of Control to Streamlined and Successful** at your favorite bookstore.

[3] If you are living in overwhelm because you say yes to everything and everybody, please watch the **Six Ways to Say No to Others so You Can Say Yes To Yourself** workshop recording at the Women Lead Movement online found at **CoachBethCaldwell. com**.

[4] Find my favorite aromatherapy scents in the resource section of this book.

[5] When working with therapists, mental health professionals or any healing practitioner, take your time and choose wisely. Your emotional health is an important part of your overall well being. Don't choose someone because of price or location. Ask for recommendations. Seek an established professional that offers compatibility, specific experience, and positive results.

Your inner voice will never lead you in the wrong direction.

Chapter Eight
Essential Intuition

Children naturally trust their instincts. As a child, you were likely comfortable using intuition. You knew instinctively if you would enjoy a sport or musical instrument and were drawn to the kinds of games and activities that brought you joy. At some point, though, we were all taught to trust facts instead of feelings.

In early history, women's intuition was highly regarded and respected in many cultures. Over the centuries, the ability to make decisions based on feelings and instincts has become feared, ridiculed and even outlawed. It's not been until very recently in our history that women have been comfortable talking about and using their intuition.

Intuition is the ability to know something without specific proof. Medical professionals and scientists have conflicting beliefs about whether intuition actually exists. Some believe that intuition can be rationalized, saying that women are more in touch with their emotions, more empathetic, more observant and more communicative than men. Therefore, women naturally make instinctual decisions, not intuitive ones. Other professionals insist that intuition is real, pointing to scientific studies showing that the corpus callosum part of the brain is thicker in females than it is in males. This thickness gives women the ability to integrate emotions, gut feelings and both hemispheres of the brain during the decision making process.[1]

A research study on the topic of intuition done by the National Institute of Mental Health proved that when faced with risk or danger, subjects were able to actually sense fear both physically and emotionally.[2]

The US Office of Naval Research believes in the potential of intuition. They are conducting studies to help marines and sailors learn to use gut instincts to have an extra edge in decision making when faced with life-threatening situations[3].

When someone tells me that they doubt the existence of intuition, I ask them, "Have you ever experienced a sixth sense or gut feeling?" Everyone has experienced these kinds of feelings at least once in their life. Some men have been highly praised for it. Here are some famous examples of men that trusted their guts and made history:

Walt Disney listened to his inner voice and created Disneyland despite difficult obstacles and overwhelming criticism.

* * *

Joseph from the old testament trusted his inner voice many times during his life. Imagine how he must have felt when following his feelings to falsely accuse his brothers of thievery! Happily, his instinct that his brothers would prove worthy was correct.

* * *

In 1914, **Henry Ford's** company was failing. Plagued by constant turnover and high demand for new cars, he did something that his peers believed to be crazy. He made the drastic decision to double wages. Within a year, turnover was reduced and production had more than doubled. He took a risk by listening to his gut instinct and it paid off.

* * *

If you do a Google search today of "famous men who have made history by trusting their gut instincts", you'll find many

78

more examples of men throughout history and modern times. Sadly, if you do the same exact search for women, you'll find only self-help articles.

When it comes to important decisions at home or work, how do you feel about trusting your intuition? If you're unsure, you're not alone. Men and women both feel that making decisions without relying on facts is risky. This is what we have been taught to believe.

My suggestion is that you include both feelings and facts when making important decisions, but always trust your inner voice, especially when it is warning you.

Have you ever had a bad feeling about a job applicant, decided to hire them anyway and then regretted your decision? Ever had that happen with someone you were dating? Security expert Gavin de Becker believes that intuition is the one and only weapon available known to prevent violent crimes. He is the author of the book **The Gift of Fear**. The examples that he shares are compelling.[4]

I have instinctively trusted my intuition for as long as I can remember. I don't rely on intuition entirely or use it to make every decision, but I have learned to trust it. Here are some examples of other women leaders who do the same:

Oprah Winfrey trusted what she calls her still, small inner voice when moving to Chicago to take a new job, even though her boss warned that it would be the end of her career. She became the most famous woman on TV. Oprah credits her intuition for the most important choices in her life.

* * *

Joan of Arc trusted her inner voice so much that, at age 16, she took her father to court to fight the marriage he had arranged. The year was 1428. She won.

79

***

In 1953, **Estee Lauder** was disrupting the cosmetics industry with her successful marketing techniques. Her competition, all men, mocked her when she gave her lipstick colors actual names like Duchess, Crimson, All-Day Rose, and Dancing Red. They warned that she'd go out of business by allowing women to try before they buy with free samples and complimentary makeovers. When the company announced a new incentive called "gift with purchase," they told her she was ridiculous and would surely go bankrupt. She remained strong and trusted her instincts. That year, Estee became the richest self-made woman in the world.

***

When **Indra Nooyi** became CEO of PepsiCo in 2006, she had her job cut out for her. She had already led the company through significant change and was receiving harsh criticism from leaders within. Unlike her predecessors who focused on immediate profits, Indra was planning for long-term success. Her controversial decision to create health-conscious products was ridiculed, but she felt strongly that this was the right move. Analysts mocked her for trying to make convenience food healthy. They called her "Mother Teresa" and they didn't mean it as a compliment. Success wasn't instant, but since 2016, the company continues to beat revenue expectations. The healthier snack options launched by Indra like Naked Juice, Cheese Stars, and Yogurt Crisps continue to perform well.

***

If you'd like to tap into your own intuition, here are some practical tips:

1. **Quiet your environment.** You can't hear you inner voice through chaos. Begin with some quiet time in the morning, evening, or when you're in the car. You'll have a lot of thoughts at first, but try to think of nothing. If you're used to constant noise, silence may be uncomfortable. Try this for about two or three minutes

at first, then increase the time gradually.

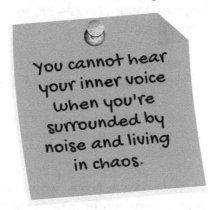

You cannot hear your inner voice when you're surrounded by noise and living in chaos.

2. **Pay attention to your thoughts.** As you practice quieting your mind, pay attention to the thoughts that come to you. Keep a tablet or another way to write notes near you so, you can record what's important. If you remember your dreams when you wake, write those down too. Eventually, you may notice patterns or discover that your subconscious is trying to tell you something.

3. **Slow your breathing.** A few times throughout the day, pause and breath deeply. Try and slow your breaths to a count of eight as you breathe in and again as you breathe out.

4. **Clear the clutter from your life.** Clutter in our homes, cars and brains can cause anxiousness and feelings of overwhelm. If your space is clutter-filled, make a plan to put things in order. Take it one room at a time or just get started with one section of a room. Then move to the next space, and so on. Realize that if you have small children, chaos and clutter come with the territory. The clutter that comes with young children is temporary. The best option is to have one clean quiet place where you can relax for now.

5. **Consider taking a class** or reading a book about mindfulness, meditation, feng-shui, yoga, chakra balancing, or Qigong.

6. **Try a guided meditation.** You can find them in most bookstores, in many apps, or on YouTube.

7. **Art projects** and some crafts can be relaxing and meditative. Consider drawing, painting, zentangle, clay, pottery or ceramics.

8. **When possible, sit near a fire or water element.** Being around fire or moving water is both meditative and relaxing. A fire could be a candle, indoor fireplace or campfire. Water can be a bubble bath, fountain, stream, lake or your favorite outdoor body of water. One of my favorite things to do is hike to local waterfalls.[5]

9. **For some people exercise is very relaxing.** A lot of people clear their heads by running, walking, playing tennis, shooting basketball or any favorite sport. One I've just learned about is called dancing mindfulness.

Trust your inner voice and use it alongside common sense. When I look back at the biggest mistakes of my life, my inner voice warned me 100% of the time but I didn't listen. Intuition is a gift that can lead you to amazing insights. Anything is possible. What's possible for you?

[1] **Forbes Magazine,** "The Science Behind Intuition", February 2, 2017

[2] To learn more about research on intuition being done by the National Institute of Mental Health visit www.ncbi.nlm.nih.gov/pubmed/9036851.

[3] To learn more about research on intuition being done by

the US Military visit www.onr.navy.mil/en/Media-Center/Press-Releases/2014/ONR-studies-intuitive-decision-making.

[4] Gavin de Becker's book is called **The Gift of Fear** and can be found in any bookstore. Get a sneak peek at the content here: www.oprah.com/relationships/trusting-your-intuition-could-save-your-life/all.

[5] To see my recent hike to a waterfall and an important lesson I learned, go to **CoachBethCaldwell.com**. Click on the Women Lead Movement and look for the video titled **Lessons I Learned from a Goose.**

When you stop living in reactive mode
you can finally enjoy a life that you
don't need a vacation from.

Chapter Nine
Living and Leading with Intention

In December, 2014 I had just hired a new life coach. I was anxious to share my goals for the upcoming new year with her. She listened patiently as I read off my list of unrealistic expectations. I was demanding accountability from myself and I expected her to hold me accountable as well. My resolutions were filled with shoulds, musts and never-agains. I was excited and thrilled with it. She was quiet.

"It seems a little extreme," she said.

"Not at all," I insisted.

Even though I had a successful business, just had my 7th book published, was about to head off to the largest speaking platform of my career and was raising two young men alone, I was determined to stop slacking.

"Beth, if you could sum up all of these goals into one word, what would that word be?"

I was stumped.

She went on to tell me about the one word movement. My assignment was to research the movement and choose my one word theme for the year. I learned that the movement was created to prevent people from beating themselves up year after year with unrealistic New Year's Resolutions. The premise is to choose a theme for yourself that encompasses who you want to be and how you want to feel in the following areas of your life:

- Career
- Physical Health/Fitness
- Emotional/Mental Health
- Friends

- Finance
- Wellness and Nutrition
- Family
- Spiritual Life

I fell in love with the movement but typical overachiever that I was back then, I could not stick to one word, so I chose two. My first "one-word" was actually two, **Clarity and Release.** I wanted clarity to realize all of the things I needed to stop doing and the ability to release the tasks that I was hanging onto, so I thought these words worked well together.

I don't recommend choosing two words. If I were to do that year over I would have chosen one word for a few months and another word after that. I was so rigid and intense back then that I thought I had to wait an entire year before choosing a new word. That's not how it works.

Embrace a one-word theme until you fulfill that desire. Then, choose another theme. The time period is not a requirement. You don't have to wait until January to choose a theme. You can make this choice at anytime.

Here are the one-word themes that I have used over the past few years:

- Clarity
- Empowered
- Intentional
- Ascend

- Release
- Abundance
- Leverage
- Delight

Some of my clients have chosen these themes:

- Flow
- Happy

- Vibrant
- Serene

- Pioneer
- Passion
- Joy
- Thrive
- Intuition
- Love
- Trust
- Purpose
- Presence
- Fun
- Optimism

- Influence
- Simplify
- Grace
- Calm
- Contented
- Bloom
- Conscious
- Creative
- Phenomenal
- Capable
- Peace

Notice that these types of words ARE NOT USED:

- Focus
- Lean
- Discipline
- Systemize
- Improve
- Sacrifice

- Organized
- Structure
- Stretch
- Determined
- Resolve
- Reduce

Negative and harsh words are not helpful. The idea is for you to enjoy the process of aligning your life and work with your desired outcomes. It's designed so you can feel rewarded and excited about your intentions, instead of frustrated and disappointed with your resolutions.[1]

Becoming intentional has completely changed the way I make decisions and live my life. My clients have responded in the same way. Here is a simple example of how to use a one-word theme instead of a goal:

You've decided to lose weight this year. Your plan looks something like this:

- Ten glasses of pure water every day- NO SODA, NO COFFEE, NO ICED COFFEE, NO SWEET TEA
- Thirty minutes of exercise every day BEFORE BREAKFAST

- NO SUGAR
- NO CARBS
- NO ALCOHOL

This list focuses on can'ts, musts and shoulds. You're telling yourself, "If I'm going to lose weight, this is going to be hard work. Tasty foods are out. No more fun, girl, this is serious. You've slacked and you're going to pay for it now."

Can you understand why most people give up within a few weeks? Being intentional asks you to focus on your WHY, instead of the SHOULDS.

Why do you want to lose weight? Is it to look great in a dress, to stop having stiff and achy joints, to have more energy, to enjoy better health? Think of a word that describes THOSE FEELINGS. An example is:

Now, instead of thinking "no sugar" or "more water" picture the word ENERGIZED. When you're hungry, ask yourself, "Which choice will energize me, a fruit salad or half a pizza?"

When you are bored, ask, "Which activity will energize me, taking a walk or taking a nap?"

A one-word theme can help you live the life you want without frustration, disappointment, harsh criticism, self-punishment and unrealistic goals.

As you begin to practice intentional living, it will be very natural for you to bring intention into your workplace. Can you imagine workdays spent accomplishing meaningful work instead of reacting to problems all day long?

Here are some traits and characteristics of intentional leaders:

Intentional Leaders know how to Keep the Main Thing the Main Thing.

- Understanding of their roles
- Usually present and focused
- Awareness of their skills and abilities
- Confidence in their skills
- Enjoy their work
- Openness to feedback and new ideas
- Attention to the things that matter
- Feel good about what they've accomplished each day
- Trust others to do their own work
- Treat others as team members rather than subordinates
- Speak up when something is wrong
- Take responsibility for mistakes
- Do not take failure or criticism personally
- Are unfazed by drama
- Expect everyone to participate fully and share their opinions and concerns openly
- Create teams of people with diverse and complementary skills
- Recognize the achievements of others and don't need to take the credit or be the center of attention
- Have a team of dedicated and loyal employees

The best example of intentional leadership that I know is Arianna Huffington, former owner of Huffington Post, now the CEO of ThriveGlobal. She has stayed true to her intuition and been intentional throughout her career. Learning first hand the importance of sleep through her own health issues, Arianna insisted that naps be allowed during the workday and had nap rooms installed throughout the company. She encourages her employees to nurture their intuition, prioritize their health, value their time as a precious commodity and disconnect often to decompress and recharge. No one is expected to work after hours or on weekends. Employees are encouraged to have books on their nightstand instead of electronic devices. Ariana wants to create a culture of creative sustainability rather than chronic burnout, not just at her company but for all companies. Hopefully other companies will take note because her methods have paid off. She sold Huffington Post for $300 million and now pursues her passion of trying to stop the stress and burnout pandemic with a new platform called ThriveGlobal.[2]

If you want to become a more intentional person at home and at work, here are some steps to get you started:

1. Continue to develop yourself personally and professionally using books, courses, workshops and retreats. Register for at least one new course each year.

2. Prioritize your own health, wellness and nutrition. Encourage workplace wellness programs and discourage constant availability and burnout.

3. Think about ways to add value to your company and team, rather than staying stuck in problem-solving mode.

4. Spend time with like-minded leaders often. This will help to feed your soul and keep you encouraged. If they

don't exist in your workplace, connect with them outside of work. It's important to have others who share your beliefs and support you.[3]

5. Replace judgment with curiosity. Ask questions, pay close attention to others and be a great listener.

6. Include quiet time in your schedule every day so that you can think and reflect without interruption.

7. Trust yourself to make the best choices and trust your employees to do the same.

Intentional leaders weren't all born that way. Like you, they learned and improved along the way.

Think about the leader you want to become. Choose your one-word, create your intentions, and trust yourself. Imagine the possibilities. I can't wait to see what you accomplish now.

[1] To download a list of ideas for your one-word theme, visit **CoachBethCaldwell.com** and click on the **Women Lead Movement.** There you can download the same choices that I share at my client retreats.

[2] Get your free subscription to the **ThriveGlobal** newsletter here: thriveglobal.com, and read my blog on **ThriveGlobal** here: thriveglobal.com/authors/beth-caldwell.

[3] To see a list of leadership retreats and workshops that I host, refer to the resources section at the back of this book.

Your body and soul are speaking to you all the time. Are you listening?

Chapter Ten
Appreciate Wisdom

As we age, wisdom is something we begin to appreciate more. It's satisfying to be able to choose what's right for us instead of obsessing over what we didn't do, should do or could have done better.

I'm open about sharing the lessons I've learned in life and at work. I don't see any reason to have to learn these lessons on our own. Collectively, we can do much better when we share what we've learned. Not only does this save time and grief, but it creates something that humans yearn for, a sense of belonging.

The workplaces I visit often include five generations of workers. It's very rewarding to be among a diverse group of leaders who openly share their experiences in the hopes of helping each other succeed at work and enjoy life. We are all in this together, after all.

If you're wondering if you have any wisdom, trust me, you do. Think about the difficult things you've overcome, both in your personal life and career. What lessons have these experiences taught you? Have you ever had a lesson that kept appearing?

Have you ever said to yourself, "When will I learn?"

Well, THAT is your wisdom.

Here are some of my most important life lessons:

1. I'm not here to rescue everyone.

2. I don't have to be liked by everyone.

3. Even if my family criticizes me, they love me and want the best for me.

4. I'm not like everyone else and I'm not supposed to be.

5. It's ok to be different.

6. Comparing myself to others is a waste of time. I have no idea if they are truly happy anyway.

7. I cannot control the choices and actions of others.

8. No matter how much I try, I can't change or improve people.

9. Working part time doesn't mean I'm lazy.

10. If I'm feeling anxious and worried or having trouble sleeping, I've probably been working too much and I need a break.

11. The world is not filled with competition. There is room for everyone to be successful.

12. The world is full of people who need love and problems that need to be fixed. We all need each other and are not meant to depend solely on ourselves.

13. Illness is often caused by mistreating oneself. The human body is not designed to work 15 hour days.

14. Before it breaks down, the human body will give warning signs.

15. It's important to accept help as easily as I offer it.

16. Most people are doing the best they can.

17. Everything doesn't have to be done today.

18. Sleep is very important.

If you want to cultivate wisdom for yourself, here are some ideas:

- Write down some of the most difficult situations that you've experienced and list the lessons that those experiences have taught you.

- Trust yourself, even when you are stepping out of your comfort zone.

- Alongside your to-do list, create a to-stop-doing list.

- If you're old enough to read this book, there is someone younger than you who can benefit from your mentorship. Helping them will help you realize how wise you are.

- Remind yourself that you're a work in progress.

- Start a gratitude journal[1] to realize your many blessings.

- Get to know someone before you judge them.

To cultivate wisdom among others, consider hosting wisdom gatherings in your community. Share experiences, lessons, books, etc. This will help you to facilitate self-awareness and allow participants to openly talk about and explore life lessons in a supportive environment.

Being a wise woman is the complete opposite of being Wonder Woman. Wonder Woman flies all over the planet rescuing others. Wise women save themselves first then shine all day long, right where they are, attracting others to them. She doesn't rush to rescue. Instead, a wise woman inspires, encourages and supports those around her, empowering them to save themselves.

Shine on, girlfriend.

[1] My favorite book about gratitude is called **365 Thank Yous: The Year a Simple Act of Daily Gratitude Changed My Life** by John Kralik. I've read it several times and often give this book as a gift. Buy it at any bookstore.

An influential woman is one who inspires possibilities.

Chapter Eleven
Influence and Impact

You've been learning a lot about improving yourself as a leader. In this book we've covered strategies including productivity, resilience, confidence, negotiation and improving work environment. You've also learned concepts about mindfulness, trusting your intuition, cultivating wisdom and leading with intention. That's a lot of learning, and it's in addition to what you've already learned in your career, the life lessons you've acquired and the knowledge you've been collecting on your own.

Remember, you are a work in progress and you're improving all the time. Also, the place you are in your life today only exists right now. The future is filled with unlimited potential and possibilities for you.

Here are some real-life examples to inspire you:

The Taliban took over her town in Pakistan when she was young and made it illegal for girls to go to school. At age 15, **Malala Yousafzai** publicly spoke out against the Taliban, advocating for educational rights for girls. The Taliban responded by having her shot in the head. Malala was critically injured but she survived. She now lives in England and has become a world-respected activist for educational rights of women. In 2014, at age 17, Malala became the youngest ever recipient of the Nobel Peace Prize.

* * *

After reading a column in the **Pittsburgh Dispatch** newspaper stating that women were a monstrosity and the United States should consider female infanticide to deal with the growing problem, a young woman wrote an anonymous scathing reply to the editor. He was so impressed that he printed the letter and invited the writer to come into the office. It was 1885 and 16 year old Elizabeth Cochran became a reporter for the paper, allowing her to earn money to support herself, her two brothers and their widowed mother. At that time, women wrote under assumed names. She chose the name **Nellie Bly**. With no formal education, Nellie became a world famous reporter. While she is best known for her brave reporting that exposed horrible living conditions in mental institutions, Nellie also did other important work including foreign correspondence in Mexico and famously reporting on a trip where she traveled around the world in 72 days. Later, she served as the first female reporter on the Eastern Front in World War I. Passionate about finding improvements to make work and life easier, she received patents for her inventions.[1] Her courage and confidence were examples to other women of the time. Nellie died just two years after women earned the right to vote.

* * *

At eight years old, she was a refugee. With the help of the Hebrew Immigrant Aid Society, her family escaped genocide. They fled from their hometown of Kiev, Russia and were relocated to Milwaukee, Wisconsin. A brave, independent and strong-willed girl, **Golda Meir** learned English and graduated at the top of her grade school class. Even as a young girl, she recognized the importance of education to impoverished families and immigrants. At age 10, Golda created her own organization to raise money and buy textbooks for young children. At age 14 she ran away from home because her father did not see the need for her to continue her education and wanted her to marry. She stayed with a sister until her father agreed to let her attend high school. Golda did eventually marry but also dedicated her life to establishing a New Zion for her people. She became the second Prime Minister of Israel. Golda advised other leaders, "Make the most of yourself by fanning the tiny, inner sparks of possibility into flames of achievement."

* * *

These women[2] and all of the women whose stories I've shared in this book have something in common with you: They were not afraid to be different, not satisfied to settle, overcame many obstacles and wanted to make the world a better place. You are no different. You can also have a great impact and influence others. I believe that you will.

Take a moment to think about the work you're doing at home, in your career or in the community. See your life as it is right now. Focus on that vision for a moment. It will never again be as it is today. Your children are growing and will one day create lives of their own. Your company and community will go on without you when you're gone. There will be a time when you're no longer on the planet. When that time comes, what will you have left behind? When you're gone, what will people remember about you? What will be your legacy?

Please, for the world's sake, don't be remembered because you really knew how to load a dishwasher efficiently or had everyone's sock drawer immaculately organized. You're here for a much more important reason.

We have many opportunities available to us today, the kind that our mothers and grandmothers had no access to. What kind of influence do you want to be?

That is your gift, your destiny, your influence and you're impact.

Yes, you can.

[1] Read about Nellie Bly's inventions and how they impacted the kitchenware and oil and gas industries here: aoghs.org/transportation/nellie-bly-oil-drum.

[2] To read more about women who will inspire you, check out nytimes.com/interactive/2018/obituaries/overlooked.html and womenshistory.org/womens-history/stories.

Chapter Twelve

Resources

To receive my weekly newsletter that includes practical tips for life and business, along with some inspiration and my newest favorite finds, visit my website **CoachBethCaldwell.com** and look for the link to sign up for the **Friday Focus.**

For daily inspiration and motivation, join my Facebook Group here:
facebook.com/groups/
mondaymorningmastermindwithbethcaldwell.

To read my blog on ThriveGlobal, visit this link: **thriveglobal. com/authors/beth-caldwell.**

To learn about the next Leadership Academy for Women, visit **Womens-Leadership-Academy.com.**

The other resources mentioned in this book are listed below. Additional resources including videos can be found at CoachBethCaldwell.com. Click on the tab called **Women Lead Movement.**

Sample Voice Message Greetings

A voice message greeting is often the first impression you'll make. I want you to sound clear and confident with no background noise. Remember, NO APOLOGIZING! While recording this, imagine that a television producer is listening attentively. Here are some examples:

Hi, you've reached the office of (your name, your title, your company name). Please leave a message after the tone.

- - -

Hello, this is (your name, your title, your company name). For immediate service, contact (alternative contact person or information here). Or, leave a message and I'll return your call by end of business today.

For Vacation or Leave Situations

Hi, you've reached (your name, your title, your company name) It's a (boy/girl)! I'll be returning from maternity/paternity leave on (date). In the meantime, contact (alternative contact information). I look forward to reconnecting with you in (name the month you'll be back, not the day).

- - -

Hello, this is (your name, your title, your company name). I'm out of the office until (vacation return date). For assistance before I return, contact (co-worker name and contact information). Otherwise, I look forward to returning your call (the week of your return).

Sample Professional Email Signature Lines

Just as your voice message greeting, you want your email signature line to be poised, professional and confident. Most email providers allow you to include a photo and website link in your signature line. It can look something like one of these:

Beth Caldwell
Life and Leadership
Coach for Women
(412) 202-6983

Ruthann Bowen
Chief Marketing Officer | Sales + Marketing
Eastcamp Creative
724-991-1934
ruthann@eastcampcreative.com
eastcampcreative.com
Click to Schedule a free 15 minute call

with Beth Caldwell

Tracie O'Neil
Medical Intuitive &
Traditional Naturopath
Having trouble sleeping?
Click here:
divinehealthnaturally.com/healthandwellness/divinesleeptips

If you'd like to use a professional service, the one I use is **WiseStamp.com**. Another option that many of my clients use is **hubspot.com/email-signature-generator**.

Writing and Productivity Resources

My favorite Grammar-checking software is **grammarly.com**.

My favorite website blocking software is **selfcontrolapp.com**.

Creativity Resources

My favorite one-word website is **getoneword.com**.

Read more about Dancing Mindfulness here: **dancingmindfulness.com**.

Essential Oils

Aromaland is an independently owned company based in Santa Fe, New Mexico that offers 100% pure therapeutic essential oils. My favorite aromatherapy scents from Aromaland are Inspiration Blend, Goddess, and Enchantment. I diffuse these oils to make my office smell divine and help me to tap into my creativity. Shop at **aromaland.com** or call 800-933-5267.

I also frequently use dōTERRA® essential oils and often receive them as gifts. dōTERRA is a multi-level marketing company founded in 2008 by a group of health care and business professionals. Their products can be ordered online or through distributors. I use a number of dōTERRA oils, and will apply them directly on my skin as well as diffusing them throughout my home and office.

Here are my favorites:

Balance is great to keep calm before a presentation.

Console helped me recover from the loss of my dad.

Peace is absolutely beautiful and I use it during hectic times to stay grounded.

InTune helps me to get focused and stay on track with writing projects.

Wild Orange is a wonderful scent to diffuse in your office. dōTERRA leader Amy Widmer tells me that orange is the scent of prosperity and abundance.

I always keep **Breathe, DigestZen** and **OnGuard** oils with me for natural solutions to sinus issues, indigestion or when I need immune support. If you see me at an event, ask to see my oil bag!

To speak to an aromatherapy expert, contact Amy Widmer at **lightpathwellness.com/about**.

My Favorite Books

The books I keep on my nightstand to read over and over again are:

The War of Art by Steven Pressfield
SH*T The Moon Said by Gerard Armond Powell
The Art of Having it All by Christy Whitman

Any time I need inspiration I will reach for one of these three books. I've read the chapters over and over again and seem to always gain a different and fresh perspective each time.

Favorite Podcasts

If I'm driving in the car, chances are I'm listening to a podcast. These are my favorites:

Glambition with Ali Brown - This is a class-act podcast with high quality content. Ali interviews women who are enjoying success and living on their own terms. She does a fantastic job of gathering women together and showing them what is possible.

Entrepreneurs on Fire with John Lee Dumas - This was the first podcast I listened to, and my first subscription. John's podcasts have been inspiring me for years. Every single day he offers quality content and interesting interviews with successful entrepreneurs.

The Life Coach School with Brooke Castillo - This podcast has done so much more than entertain and inspire me. The self-coaching tools that I've learned from Brooke's podcast have changed my life and helped me set and achieve intentions that I never before dreamed of.

Rich Coach Club with Susan Hyatt - My go-to-listen when I want to remind myself of the power that we all hold within ourselves. Susan is unapologetically true to her beliefs. She dreams big and has inspired me to do the same.

Leadership Retreats and Workshops

To learn about upcoming Leadership Workshops and Women's Retreats visit **womens-leadership-academy.com** and click on events.

Beth Caldwell's
BRAND YOU REVIEW
CHECKLIST

☐ Clear and Confident Voice Message

☐ Complete Email Signature Line

☐ Recent Professional Photo

☐ Compelling Short Bio/Introduction

☐ Updated "About" Page on Website

☐ Updated Membership Listings

☐ Updated Community Service Positions

☐ List of Potential Awards

☐ List of Media Opportunities

☐ Writing Opportunities

☐ Speaking Opportunities

Beth Caldwell's
AWKWARD CONVERSATION
STRATEGIES

1. I don't want to monopolize your time.

2. I disagree. I've always found Susan to be...

3. Let's get back on topic.

4. That's an interesting perspective.

5. You've given me something to think about.

6. This topic is obviously very important to you.

7. No time for a debate right now.

8. Fascinating. Excuse Me.

Beth Caldwell's
CONFLICT CONVERSATION
STRATEGIES

1. First, decide your acceptable outcome.

2. Begin by reassuring.

3. Clarify meeting end time.

4. State the obvious problem.

5. Share the acceptable outcome.

6. Empathize with fears.

7. Understand the motivations of others.

8. End on time.

30 days to a
clutter free
email in-box

30 Days to a Clutter-Free Email In-Box

If your email in-box is out of control and you want to clean it up, you don't have to do it all at once. It's very much like an attic, garage or basement that's been allowed to get filled with clutter. You could spend an entire Saturday working hard, feeling exhausted and drained when it's done, or you can spend 5-15 minutes a day and have it organized and looking good in 30 days.

Here is how I did it:

Day One:
Archive any emails that are more than 1 year old. You can do this by creating folders on your desktop or shared drive. Follow the instructions from your email service provider on how to download or archive emails. Create a separate folder for each year. This will remove the emails from your inbox but still keep them available. If you need to search for something you'll know exactly where to find it.

Day Two:
Delete and unsubscribe from any email subscriptions that don't provide value. Then, stop all email notifications from social media sites.

Day Three:
If you haven't already, create a separate email account for your personal emails so they remain separate from business emails.

Day Four:
Use in-box folders to simplify your business. Some people create a folder for each client. I have a folder for the industry and membership emails that I want to read but don't need to see the minute they arrive.

Days Five Through Thirty:
Spend time each of the remaining days organizing and clearing out the emails that are still inside your in-box. This is an easier task when sorting emails alphabetically by the sender. Look for the sort function at the top of you inbox. Review one letter of the alphabet at a time. Today, do the A's, tomorrow do all the B's and so on. Review these emails and decide to:

- Delete what you don't need.
- Move the to-do's onto your calendar.
- Unsubscribe from the ones you no longer want but missed on day two.

Letters like F, Q, and X will be very quick. The letters S, L, M usually take a little longer. When you're finished you'll have shifted your email overwhelm to clutter-free, streamlined and organized.

Other Books by Beth Caldwell

From Frantic to Focused: How to Shift Your Life from Out-of-Control to Streamlined and Successful

Smart Leadership: 12 Simple Strategies to Help You Shift From Ineffective Boss to Brilliant Leader

SHIFT: How to Stand Out, Be Seen and Grow Your Business With Integrity

SHIFT Success Journal

Publicity Action Plan Workbook: A Comprehensive Step-by-Step Workbook to Create a Complete Publicity Plan to Grow Your Business

Inspire: Women's Stories of Accomplishment, Encouragement and Influence

Empower: Women's Stories of Breakthrough, Discovery and Triumph

Inspired Entrepreneurs: A Collection of Female Triumphs in Business and Life

I Wish I'd Known That!: Secrets to Success in Business from Women Who've Been There

Books by Beth Caldwell are available in bookstores nationwide or your favorite online retailer. To invite Beth to speak to your book club, conference or company call (412) 202-6983.

Leadership Academy

for Women

Leadership Academy for Women, created by Beth Caldwell, is an innovative professional and personal development program for aspiring women leaders. The course is made up of ten workshops and two private coaching sessions. Leadership Academy has always been available as a group program that happens once each year. Due to the demand of travel schedules and accessibility, the course is now available to be taken privately as a one on one course. You can also invite Beth to bring Leadership Academy to your workplace.

Over twelve weeks, the course is designed to help women understand their leadership style, develop authentic leadership skills, and learn to lead others effectively. To find out more and decide if you want to attend the academy, visit **Womens-Leadership-Academy.com.**

"Leadership Academy provided me with some much needed clarity as a young woman seeking out her place in the non-profit world. Collaborating with other women in a supportive and educational space helped shape how I lead and how I work, and it wouldn't have been possible without Beth's support and guidance." **- Margot Martin, Non-Profit Development Director, Portland, Oregon**

"Even though I invested in a five year MBA at a prestigious university, Leadership Academy was without a doubt the best investment I ever made in myself." **- Katie White, New York City**

"More take-aways than I can count. I use the tools I learned in

Leadership Academy EVERY DAY in my life and business."
- Claire Schuchman, Pittsburgh, Pennsylvania

Visit The Women Lead Movement online for continued resources and inspiration from Beth Caldwell. Go to **CoachBethCaldwell.com** and click on

The Women Lead Movement.

Meet The Author

Beth Caldwell is the author of more than ten books on leadership, inspiration, and personal development. She believes that women CAN do it all, just not at the same time. She is the founder and creator of the **SHIFT Program** and **Leadership Academy for Women**. She is the former host of the popular WebTV Show **Smart Leadership** and currently hosts a motivational weekly broadcast called **Monday Morning Mastermind**.

Beth spent four years teaching with the **Steve Harvey Success Institute** on the topics of leadership, time management and personal success. She's received the **Pittsburgh Magazine** 40 Under 40 Award for being an innovative young leader and was recently honored with the **Woman of Courage Award**. Find out what she's up to next at **CoachBethCaldwell.com**.